CHASING HEARTBREAK

KAT T. MASEN

Kat T. Masen

Chasing Heartbreak

A Friends-to-Lovers Romance
The Dark Love Series Book 6

Disclaimer: The material in this book contains graphic language and sexual content and is intended for mature audiences, ages 18 and older.

ISBN: 979-8581105801
ISBN: 979-8782876579

Editing by Nicki at Swish Design & Editing
Proofing by Kay at Swish Design & Editing
Cover Image Copyright 2020
First Edition 2020
All Rights Reserved

ONE

KATE

Four Years Ago

"Two words for you... honey daddy."

Eric adjusted the lapels on his overly priced designer shirt, checked his reflection against the glass door, and complained about his hair, *again*. Distracted by his incessant rambling on styling products and a loose strand of hair refusing to cooperate, I took the opportunity to check my appearance.

Unlike Eric, my hair was correctly styled into a tight bun toward the back of my head, not a single strand out of place. The simple hairstyle suits this type of soirée—formal, with an elite guest list in a very fancy house.

And I'd only seen the front entrance.

Somehow, Eric persuaded me to attend his mother's sixtieth birthday party. It was being held at their newly purchased East Hamptons estate. According to Eric, the house was a birthday present from dear old daddy for never being home and always traveling abroad.

Some birthday present!

And, of course, the invitation came at the last minute.
Eric was supposed to bring his colleague, Emma, but she
had some sort of personal emergency. Eric narrowed it
down to being knee-deep in Italian dick, or Aunt Flow is
paying a visit. Knowing I was his backup, I didn't give in so
quickly, making him practically beg for me to attend. In
exchange for my presence, he promised to take me to this
new restaurant I had been dying to try, but because of some
waitlist, I could never get a table. He had connections, and I
took advantage of those connections to finally taste the
famous crème brûleé the chef is known for.

"Honey daddy?" I question while grimacing. "You
mean sugar daddy?"

"Sweetheart..." Eric purrs in his over-the-top fake
British accent, "... you need a man of age. Someone of matu-
rity. Honey is sweeter than sugar."

I don't question Eric any further after he lost me at man
of age. Most of the time, I let him do his thing while I
blatantly ignore his quest to find me a man. Sometimes, it's
just easier to nod my head and sidetrack him with pointless
gossip.

I'd been attending quite a number of these upscale
events in the city, so I had the perfect dress to wear—a black
off-the-shoulder maxi dress with a high slit stopping mid-
thigh. The dress was gorgeous and was an impromptu
purchase last fall when Charlie visited Manhattan,
warranting a much-needed girls' shopping trip and dent to
my credit card.

Of late, I'd worn it to three separate events. My rule is if
the guest list differs, a green light to recycle the wardrobe.
Eric hated this rule, which is why I lied and told him it was
brand new on the ride over here.

We stood in front of the large doors as the butler

answered formally. The home's sheer size was breathtaking, and only a few minutes ago, I was wowed by the front iron gates. In Eric's exact words, the home was sophisticated and a meticulously crafted estate sitting only minutes away from the harbor. I swore he pulled those words from an architectural digest of some sort. His usual responses were, 'this is a palace fit for a queen like myself,' or in some cases, 'what a shithole, I wouldn't send my ex here, and that's saying a lot since he's pure trash.'

Once we had passed the gated entry and elegantly landscaped grounds, I knew Eric wasn't joking when he said the house was enormous. He'd only been here once since his father purchased it. Yet he made it quite clear he planned to spend his summer vacation lounging by the pool while being served by a butler and eyeing the pool boy who happened to be a confused straight guy fresh out of college.

We took a step into the open foyer, and my eyes immediately gazed up toward the high ceilings and intricate detail. In proper Hamptons design, each room boasted high ceilings, massive windows, custom cabinetry, and bespoke leather accents. I loved architecture and design, wishing I'd studied it in school since it's my passion.

"This house is... wow, that fireplace is stunning," I raved, taking small steps while admiring the décor.

"I know, right?" Eric smiled politely at guests who walked past and kept his arm linked with mine. "My mother has exquisite taste."

"Yeah, and Daddy has a nice checking account."

Eric snickered as we continued to walk through the wide hallway toward the back French doors. Everywhere I turned, my eyes admired the detailed pieces from the chandeliers to the sconces. We strolled past the open-plan kitchen with marble countertops, so grand in its presence and equipped with every appliance a chef would need.

We stopped at the doors which were open to the enormous yard. Directly in front of us was an Olympic-sized swimming pool, and although Charlie and Lex's place had quite a large pool, this one was even grander. For someone who grew up in England, pools always fascinated me.

With dusk setting in, the lights were turned on and illuminated the crystal-clear blue water, making the pool mesmerizing with its calming nature.

The trees surrounding us were dressed in fairy lights, brightening the outdoor area and giving it a whimsical feel. Toward the right, across a sizable makeshift dance floor, a small band was playing 1950's music, which, according to Eric, is his mother's favorite era.

"Eric, darling, you came."

A woman, assuming it was his mother judging by the similar facial features, was dressed in a beautiful blush couture gown with a diamond necklace draped around her neck. When I first met him, Eric told me that his mother was of Chinese descent and his father was a full-blooded white American. Together, it caused many issues earlier on in their relationship, but they managed to remain married for over forty years. On closer inspection, I could see where Eric got all his features from.

She kissed both of Eric's cheeks while holding his hands. With a warm smile, she let go to fix his hair just the way he liked it.

"Mom, this is Kate," Eric introduced me. "Kate, my mother, Vivian."

I leaned in to kiss both her cheeks, wishing her a happy birthday at the same time. The scent of Chanel No. 5 lingered in the air between us.

"You're just as gorgeous as my baby described you," she said with a gracious tone. "And your accent is just darling."

"I know, right? I told you, Mom. I should try to find myself a British gay man."

"Oh, Eric." She patted him gently on the chest. "Tristan will be back. You've got to give monogamy a try."

I pursed my lips and kept my smile fixed. When it came to matters of the heart, Eric refused to settle down, thinking these years were made for partying and bed-hopping. Though, somehow, he'd fallen in love yet refused to acknowledge said fact.

Basically, he's a royal pain in the ass and such a high-maintenance friend.

"I must say hello to your uncle and aunt from Boston." She cupped his chin with pleading eyes. "Please try to talk more than two words with your brother, okay?"

Eric nodded, and the second she was a fair distance away from us, he mumbled something about geeks and small dicks.

"Your mother is beautiful and so refined..." I trailed off while watching Vivian greet her guests. "What the hell happened to you?"

"Hey, I resent your judgment!"

Eric quickly switched his grumpy face to desperation as he caught a waiter serving shrimp, having complained the entire ride over here of being in starvation central. After a trying day at work with a deal that almost fell through, I was happy to drown myself in champagne and pass on the questionable sea-life with its disgusting tail limp on the silver platter. Aside from my mother's homemade fish recipe back home, I wasn't a seafood person.

"Okay, so here's the lowdown on the guests." Eric pulled me aside as if he would reveal some sort of government-kept secret and discreetly pointed to the man a few feet from us. "Ivan owns three properties in The Hamptons plus this gorgeous place in Martha's Vineyard. He runs his own wine emporium and exports to Southeast Asia or something like that."

"The man with the cravat?" I asked, watching him hold a pipe.

"Yes, the man with the cravat." Eric shuddered, his distaste for cravats needed a whole other discussion. "He's onto wife number three. Not too bad considering he looks like he belongs in a nursing home."

"Lovely," was all I answered.

"Word around Mom's tennis club is that wife number three is tapping her tennis instructor. I could get you in."

"Um, get me in where?"

"In," Eric repeated, eyes wide, making some weird gesture with his hands. "In his bed and bank account."

Cocking my head, I shook it with annoyance. "I don't need a man, let alone one who could pass as my great-grandfather."

"Okay, fine," Eric sniped. "The guy over there in the burgundy suit..."

"You mean the *velvet* burgundy suit?" I pointed out, knowing just how much Eric hated velvet.

"Never mind the wardrobe. Thiago is second in line to his grandfather's estate, which happens to be the most expensive piece of real estate in the Bahamas. Plus, he designs handbags for a living."

"He designs handbags?" I questioned and grabbed another champagne from the waiter who passed us by. "I think that's more up your alley. And besides, second in line isn't exactly first in line."

I don't even know why I entertained this conversation.

Firstly, I didn't need a man, and even if I did, I could find one myself. Secondly, Eric was the worst at trying to set people up. His idea of date-worthy wasn't exactly the same as mine.

"And wait," I add, feeding my curiosity. "How do you know all this?"

Eric shuffled his feet and lowered his head as if caught in a naughty act while hovering behind me in an odd way. "Um, no reason... through the street."

"Does the street mean you screwed him, which is why you're trying to stand behind me?"

"Fine." Eric stomped his foot and crossed his arms. "We had a moment inside a closet at a party a few years back."

"You had a moment?" I scoff as I took a sip of my champagne. "What does that even mean?"

"It means I jerked him off because he was too big to take all in."

The bubbles got caught in my throat, and a coughing fit followed as I tried to gulp for air. Just when I thought I was about to die, I managed to compose myself and control my breathing.

"Would you keep it down?" Eric hushed me and kept his gaze lowered. "He'll see us standing here."

"But I'm so confused." My voice came out uneven and breathless, forcing me to drink again to clear it. "You always talk about the bigger the dick, the better."

"Honey, we're not talking just big," Eric asserted and raised his hand toward his chest. "We're talking thick big."

"Thick big?"

Eric widened his hands, my mouth opened in shock. Indeed, he exaggerated. No one was that thick, and Eric was known to embellish girth on more than one occasion.

"All right, we're done with this conversation," I told him

as I scanned the area around us in an effort to talk about something else.

Close to Vivian, I saw a man standing beside her. I was drawn to his tall stature, the way he towered over her yet still gazed at her in a loving way. His dashing black tuxedo with his black-rimmed reading glasses made him look like an incredibly sexy Clark Kent, especially with the way his jet-black hair was perfectly styled to the side.

"And that guy over there?" I nodded in his direction.

Eric exhaled while he rolled his eyes of boredom. "That's my brother, Dominic. I'm surprised he knows how to pull a tux off. Don't even bother saying hello. You might as well talk to a brick wall."

Well, if truth be told, the brick wall was beautiful. Dominic looked nothing like Eric—much taller with lighter skin and features. From where I was standing, his hair looked like the only similar thing to Eric—jet-black and straight. Aside from that, you wouldn't pick them as siblings.

"Oh, listen." Eric's mood shifted, and his tone picked up with excitement. "Mom is talking to that lady from the *Real Housewives*, you know, the bitchy one, but she's Celine Dion's second cousin. Or something like that."

"Eric, you know I don't watch television, let alone reality TV."

"Right, right," he mumbled, distracted. "I'll be back."

When Eric says he'll be back, I'm pretty much guaranteed to be alone for most of the night. Why I agreed to this again is beyond me. *You have no life outside of work, that's why*.

With my champagne in hand, the last remnants went down too quickly while I stood on the patio and watched the night sky. There was a peacefulness to being out of the city, away from the hustle and bustle, and able to clearly see each star. It reminded me of back home, bringing on nostalgia and memories of what felt like a lifetime ago.

The area around me began to get crowded and prompted me to find a quieter place. I took a walk in the gardens with great difficulty as my heels dug into the perfect lawn and away from the noise to enjoy the peace and quiet. The sky was even more visible away from the party, every star shined brightly above me with a glimpse of one shooting in the distance. The proximity of the sea provided a fresh breeze, cooling down the warm summer night.

"Care for a top-up?"

The voice startled me. Clutching my chest, I turned to find Dominic standing beside me, carrying his own bottle of liquor. I'd considered myself a reasonably tall woman if compared to Charlie or Adriana, but Dominic towered over me, much like Lex.

"Why, thank you." I smiled politely and ignored Eric's words and noticed the label on the bottle—Dom Perignon.

"Dominic Kennedy."

"Kate Hamilton," I followed and extended my hand to shake his. "Yes, your brother has um..."

"Warned you to stay away?" He snickered with a disturbing laugh. "Referred to me as weird geek with no personality? Actually, to be precise, a brick wall would be more fitting."

"Eric wouldn't say that," I lied.

"You're not the best of liars."

"I'm not lying." I almost busted out laughing at this incredibly gorgeous stranger and hid my smile behind my glass. "Perhaps an extension of the truth is more on point. Besides, Eric is complicated."

Isn't that the goddamn truth?

"He dragged you to this?"

"He didn't have to twist my arm or anything. It's not like I was busy." I cover my mouth again as a slight cough escapes me. Telling Dominic I wasn't busy is the same as telling him I'm single, wide open for anything, literally. "It's all work and no play these days."

Dominic pursed his lips with a slight nod. He motioned to me to follow him to a secluded part of the garden with beautiful trees surrounding us and an old oak chair.

"Sit, please." He gestured.

I took a seat, pushing the bottom of my dress aside to avoid it getting caught in my heels. As I sat beside him, the smell of his cologne was intoxicating—masculine with a hint of dominance—or maybe it was forever since I smelled a man so good, and even longer since I last slept with anyone. My mind did a mental calculation, but the numbers went too far back that I can't even compute. No wonder Eric and Charlie were always trying to set me up on dates. My personal life was beyond tragic.

Silence crept up between us, and only the rustle of the trees could be heard. The only thing we had in common to discuss was Eric.

"So, I can only imagine growing up with Eric would've been fun."

"Not really."

"He's complicated." I carried on to keep the conversation flowing. "But I have to hand it to him, he knows how to have fun."

Dominic forced a smile, not looking impressed with the conversation swaying toward his brother. Okay, this was getting worse. I need to try a different angle.

"What do you do for a living?"

"A bit of this and that," he responded flatly.

"Right..." I'm tapped out. It was like pulling teeth out. How could a man so incredibly sexy be so dull? A moment ago, we had light-hearted banter, and now it's crickets. Eric may not have been so wrong in his brick-wall analogy.

I raised my glass toward my lips and downed the champagne in one go. I thought of a reason to excuse myself, and the best I could come up with was to use the bathroom, which wasn't far from the truth.

"Listen, Dominic, I, uh..."

"You're beautiful," he confessed as he poured more champagne into my glass, which caught me by surprise. "I've heard Eric speak about you to my mother. You're the CEO of the Lexed office in Manhattan."

"And London," I mumbled in an uncertain tone. "And, um, thanks for the compliment?"

Dominic laughed, the lines around his eyes creased slightly. "Too left field?"

"Left field, or maybe just wasn't expecting it. It's been a while, hearing a compliment like that. So, thank you."

"You're telling me you don't hear such compliments daily?"

"Well, not really. I spend most of my days in the office or with clients. It would be highly inappropriate to be complimented in such a way and would have a serious breach of workplace protocol. Like I said earlier, all work and no play."

"All work, no play," he repeated in a low voice. "Interesting."

"How so?" I asked, curious about his sudden interest in my personal life. "Let's be honest, Dominic, we're both adults. Working long hours then crawling back to my apartment at some godawful hour means I have no personal life. I'm not a dating person, although Eric will argue that in a heartbeat. And so, with that said, work has become my life. I don't have time for relationships unless a man understood my lifestyle, and so far, that's come up empty."

I'd laid all the cards on the table, unsure why I'd gone this far. I blamed the champagne plus my empty stomach and the combination of both of those mixed together. Add in a handsome man beside me and a raging libido, and that right there was your answer.

"What if you could have both?" he questioned with a serious tone.

"Both what?"

"Your passion, your work, and have your personal needs fulfilled?"

I laughed, shaking my head. "Then, I'd say it's my lucky day."

Dominic didn't say another word. Placing his hand in his pocket, he removed a business card, handing it to me. "Call me sometime."

Standing up, he poured the remains into my glass with a playing smirk. For a brief moment, he lingered but then walked away like a thief in the night.

Call me? Is that it?

What the hell was that?

I gave myself time to process our encounter. Undoubtedly, he could've stayed around and conversed rather than handing me a business card, mainly after I rambled on about my personal life. Then, he questioned me about all my needs being fulfilled. It's bizarre, or maybe, I was boring, and it was his way out, thinking I wouldn't have the courage to call him.

Ten minutes later, and with an empty glass, I made my

way back to the party with an over-dramatic Eric raising his hands when he sees me.

"There you are!" He sounded panicked, the high-pitched tone hurting my eardrum. "Jesus Christ, Kate, I was this close to unraveling a cravat in the pool house. Where were you?"

"Just, um..." I decided to keep my chat with Dominic to myself as it would only bore Eric, anyway. "Just walking around the grounds and admiring the property."

"Okay, way to get laid tonight," he dragged, distracted by a large birthday cake being presented to his mother. "I'll be back."

The band began to play a sweet version of Happy Birthday as the crowd sang. Eric's father stood beside Vivian, and standing on the other side were Dominic and Eric. Between them, I could see the strong gene pool with Dominic looking more like his father.

Vivian blew out the candles as we all cheered, then kissed Eric on the cheek and then Dominic. She kissed her husband with a loving smile before he turned to the mic and said a few words.

His speech was delivered with admiration and love toward his wife, and a few humorous anecdotes prompted their guests to laugh. I found myself listening attentively, but somewhere during a mention of his sons, my eyes shifted toward Dominic.

He was staring directly at me, a piercing gaze caught me by surprise and left me breathless. My rational thoughts told me to look away, yet I couldn't seem to shift my gaze, almost as if a magnetic force pulled me.

Taking a deep breath, I thought of ways to ignore Dominic. After this party was over, I no longer needed to torture myself in his presence. Nothing good would come of it, anyway. He's Eric's brother, and no matter how handsome he may be, I didn't want to ruin my friendship with Eric.

Inside my purse, I pulled out his card and re-read it.

I placed it back in my clutch as if it would magically disappear, ignoring the sensation building inside of me. You imagined all of this, conjured up wild thoughts because you lacked intimacy with a man, especially one so sexy.

I could resist his charm.

And resist the temptation to call him.

But for how long, I had no idea.

TWO

KATE

Present

There's something to be said about the change of
seasons in France.

It was only a few weeks ago when I walked
the streets, admiring the pretty pastel blossoms and the lush
green parks while over-indulging in chocolate during Easter
celebrations. People are much more pleasant, welcoming
the sunshine after a dreary winter.

But time flew by quickly, and we all found ourselves in
a much more uncomfortable predicament—summer.

Our skin burned from the summer sun, and our clothes
clung to us mixed with an uncomfortable sweat while we
fanned ourselves relentlessly for some sort of relief. Many
people are flocking to the south to bathe in the ocean, fortunate enough to vacation and not be chained to the office
like me.

I shouldn't complain though, the air conditioning is my
best friend during the sweltering heat outside.

Back in the States, the Americans will mock us English

folk for our constant complaining of the tiresome heat and dragging summers. I'm no different. My pale skin doesn't care to get sunburned, which happens way too quickly when I spend any moment unprotected under the harsh summer rays.

This is why fall is, by far, my favorite season. The air is more relaxed and bearable, yet the sun still shines through the day. At night, there's a slight crisp in the air with a promise of winter on the horizon. It's the perfect time to explore the outside nightlife without being stripped to barely any clothing or, in reverse, wearing a bulk load to protect yourself from the cold.

It's been three years since I moved to Paris with absolutely no regrets. My job, stressful with its demands, has become my sole focus. I've pushed myself in ways I never imagined possible, purposely threw myself into learning mode as Lex did his best to mentor me, given our geographical distance.

I created this routine, thriving in my purposely-organized schedule. The mornings start at four o'clock. A run around the park followed by yoga in my living room while I listen to audiobooks by well-known entrepreneurs from around the world. I ditched the romance novels a year or so ago, my guilty pleasure since becoming a blooming teen. Frankly, I don't need to read about the so-called happily-ever-after nonsense. Being single is the new black, and I refuse to be sucked into the emotional heartbreak authors often write about.

Without too much difficulty, I changed my eating habits. My diet consists of high-energizing food to give me stamina until the official workday ends. Coffee, being that I'm in Europe, is almost mandatory. My addiction is one I'll proudly own, and let's be honest, survival without it is practically impossible.

As France is surrounded by so many other beautiful countries, I have traveled more than I anticipated around Europe. Many nights in Rome and Venice, a quick flight to Berlin. Switzerland had been one of my favorites, such a beautiful country, and the lifestyle is so relaxed.

But Paris ultimately won my heart over and over again. I've heard it from many people, though never truly understood the meaning until I experienced it for myself. Paris has a charm and allure beyond most other cities, and I've visited quite a few through my adult years while working beside Lex.

Having left all my friends behind in the States, there's never a dull moment when I have the time to explore museums and architecture, high-end fashion boutiques, cafés, and quaint restaurants, all of which align the beautifully paved streets.

I never grow tired of the scenery as each season showcases the city so differently. Each architectural masterpiece becomes mesmerizing amongst the sun, the autumn leaves, and the beautiful blanketed snow. Everything feels grand in its presence, making me stop and appreciate its beauty amongst the chaos of everything around it. The Parisians rarely give the Eiffel Tower a second thought, something I learned very early on. Yet every cab ride past the iconic treasure, I reflect on my life and the beauty of being alive. It inspires me to follow my dreams and ambitions, and raise the bar in my so-called life. Paris is nothing like Manhattan, and the truth be told, I have no desire to go back to the city that never sleeps.

Eric often questions my sanity, telling me I need to get laid pronto because I'm this close to joining a nunnery.

However, he's quick to say that even nuns get their happily ever after, remembering the conversation word by word.

"Captain Vontrapp has been my fantasy ever since my mother made me watch The Sound of Music *at the age of seven." Eric sighed.*

"The dad?" I questioned, slightly disturbed by his admission.

"A powerful man falls in love with a nun. I mean, how romantic is that?"

"Yes, it's romantic," I agreed. "You fantasizing about him is not."

"Maybe you'll meet your captain in Paris. You can live happily ever after in his castle with his seven children while you sing songs of joy."

"I couldn't think of anything worse," I mumbled under my breath.

Even from across the globe, Eric still weighs in on my personal life, but I ignore him for the most part. There's no time to worry about relationships or men as my interests have shifted to museum visits and French culture. My fascination with France's history only grows as I delve deep into the genetics of what makes this city and country a worldwide attraction. If only I had been so studious in school, surprising even myself on how educated I have become as an adult.

The only thing Eric welcomes is my change in wardrobe. My tastes have become sophisticated. Unlike Charlie and Eric, I was never into designer labels, but Paris awakens that part of me. People are pursuing the streets dressed like runway models to the events I attend with no end of couture in sight. Women in Paris aren't afraid of fashion, especially the older generation. They stay in the decade, confident and fearless with their fashion choices. I've become bolder with some of my latest ensembles. With my rigorous exercise routine and healthy eating, I finally have the body I've always dreamed of without the plastic surgery society pressures women into. It gives me the confidence to wear things outside of my typical attire, and I never expected to be so in love with fashion in general.

But perhaps my greatest joy isn't the fashion, nor my new body. It's becoming a local and finally feeling like this could be home, immersing myself into life as a Parisian. I was forced to learn French, given it's the native tongue of almost all of my employees. While I still prefer to speak English, I know enough to have a simple conversation.

My love affair with Paris runs deep, and one I can talk about for hours. Eric and Charlie are very vocal in expressing their jealousy on almost every phone call we have.

As I sit in a local café enjoying this lazy Sunday morning which is a rare occurrence of late, my phone begins to ring in my pocket. Pulling it out to answer, I mouth 'thank you' to the waiter who serves my coffee along with a pastry I've been eager to try. I call it Sunday's guilty pleasure.

"Hello, Lex," I greet, noting the time back in Los Angeles. "It's late. Is everything okay?"

"I thought I'd try to catch you at a reasonable time," Lex strains, his voice stiff and unwelcoming.

"I was just served a triple shot of coffee, so shoot."

"We have a problem with Jefferson. I've had my suspicions, but we're talking big concerns."

I cross my legs, paying attention. "Please don't tell me we're talking insider trading?"

"I'm afraid so."

I let out a long-winded breath, also suspecting something of late. A few weeks ago, when things surfaced, I'd done a little digging but didn't have anything concrete to hold him accountable.

"We've invested too much money to have it fall apart now," I express, firmly. "This could be disastrous."

"You're telling me," he almost grits. "I've got legal on this and need you to be on standby this week. I know you are flying back to London on Thursday, but you may need to fly to Geneva to sort this out."

"Of course," I tell him, making a mental list of what I need to do. "I'll rearrange and shift some projects to make sure we don't fall behind on anything."

"Thank you. Fucking asshole."

"Listen, Lex, it's just after midnight for you. Get some sleep, and when you're back in the office on Monday, I'll have a contingency plan drawn up."

"Sleep?" His soft laugh echoes through the phone. "What's that foreign concept?"

"Charlie told me Addison has been a terror of late. Climbing into your bed in the middle of the night."

"There's nothing more terrifying than waking up in the middle of the night with your child standing next to you, just staring."

I laugh at the thought. "I guess those horror movies have worked against you. I'm sorry to hear it. Hopefully, she'll outgrow it soon."

"Either that or we're adopting her out... how about you take her?" he jokes half-heartedly.

"Hey, I'm good for short-time babysitting. You know my stance on having kids."

We say goodbye but not before Lex unloads other concerns that need my attention. It isn't unusual for him to contact me at all hours, or more specifically—the weekend. Together, we're a well-oiled machine. Despite his attempt to slow down, Lex is and will always be a workaholic.

The European market is entirely different than back in the States. More money to play with, therefore, more greedy assholes trying to fuck us over.

I finish my coffee and chouquette, then decide to take the more extended route home to clear my head before heading into the office despite it being Sunday.

Five hours later, I've drunk way too much caffeine and completely missed eating lunch. My nerves have become jittery, but I manage to get things sorted so Lex can breathe easier. When I look at the clock, I notice the time and reminder on my phone.

Reminder: *Blind Date—Gustave.*

I let out a frustrated groan, cursing at myself as to why I agreed to this in the first place. Just when I think of an excuse to bail, my phone rings, and it's the devil herself—Mrs. Matchmaker.

"Don't bail on this," Charlie scolds without a greeting.

"What are you? A clairvoyant now?" I answer abruptly, straightening my posture to stretch my tense muscles. "In case you don't know, something has come up with work."

"Not an excuse. I know for a fact you've been emailing Lex documents, therefore, you're on top of your work, and it's Sunday night. You owe me this."

Clenching my jaw, I close my eyes to calm my irritation. I agreed that once a year, Charlie is allowed to set me up on a blind date. When I consented to this, I recall being drunk on rum and Coke, combined with being sexually charged. But, of course, Charlie, with her overbearing ways, has held me to it.

The only reason I agreed to this date tonight is that last year's blind date wasn't too bad. Maxim was lovely and very good-looking. We went on four dates until he dropped the ball mid-dinner—he's bisexual and was looking to have an open relationship. We remained friends and still catch up for drinks every few months. On our last catchup, he introduced me to his new boyfriend, Youssef. The two of them are a match made in heaven and are fun to unwind with.

Charlie apparently met Maxim back in LA at some fashion event. When she found out he lived in Paris, and knowing I have been single forever, she put two and two together.

"Fine," I complain, opening my eyes. "Can you tell me more about Gustave?"

"No, because every time I tell you something, you forget anyway or use it as an excuse not to go."

"I do not."

"Just go on the date and report back later," she coaxed, then quickly cheers, "Good luck."

"Since you're the one setting me up, I'm going to need it."

I have to give it to Gustave. He chose a fine restaurant, which I know for a fact is difficult to get into and rather expensive.

He sits across from me, dressed nicely in a pale green

shirt and gray trousers. Without asking his age, he appears more mature with dark brown hair with a few grays near his temple. When he smiles, several creases surround his blue eyes. I'd peg him for early forties, which doesn't bother me so much these days.

Gustave peruses the wine list, keeping quiet and leaving an uncomfortable silence between us.

"*Ça vous dérange si je parle anglais?*" I ask him if we can speak English, given my exhaustion from working nonstop the last few hours. I can barely compute a sentence in English, let alone French. Clearly, the excess caffeine is wearing off.

"*Oui.*" He smiles, placing the menu down. "Do you like wine?"

"Who doesn't?" I jest, welcoming the topic.

Gustave turns out to be a food critic. Our conversation steers to only that. He offers to choose our meals, which I agree to, but Gustave's face looks less than pleased with the plate sitting in front of him when the waiter serves us.

We eat in silence, his face relatively blank with each bite he takes.

"Do you not like the food here?"

"It's mediocre," he responds flatly.

I start to wonder if people are watching us, trying to make sense of what the purpose is of us dining together since I can't. Unlike Gustave, I immensely enjoy the French delicacy and can't fault a single dish served tonight.

A plate of various cheeses is served, placed between us. In authentic French culture, cheese is consumed after the main dish but before dessert. Since I enjoy cheese, I don't see a problem with this at all.

"Cheese is a delicacy. If done right, it's the most satisfying meal," he speaks, slicing a small piece for himself.

I have no clue what to say to that but need something quick. "Cheese is rather satisfying."

Wow, Kate—electrifying.

"The smellier the cheese, the better." He raises the cheese toward my face. "Here, smell this?"

Leaning in, I take a sniff, immediately scrunching my nose at the godawful stench. "Amazing, isn't it?"

"So, you like cheese?" I nod, quick to change subjects before I fall asleep. "Tell me about your family?"

"My father owned a delicatessen and curated his own cheese. My mother worked with him for over fifty years.

"And siblings?"

"No, just me." He raises another piece of cheese, prompting me to sniff it. This one is even worse.

"And what about traveling? What do you like to do in your spare time?"

"Not much these days." A smile graces his lips, and I wait with bated breath for a funny anecdote. "*Comté vieux* is aged over six months. By far exceeds the rest of the cheeses."

This date is going downhill so fast, as I wait for anything that doesn't involve cheese. By the end of the date, I probably could've gotten a degree in cheese. Hands down, this can officially top one of the worst dates in history.

"Thanks for tonight, Gustave." I yawn forcefully, hoping he reads between the lines as he calls the waiter over and requests the bill. "I've learned a lot about cheese."

"It was a pleasure, Kate." Gustave kisses both my cheeks to say goodbye. "Shall I call you tomorrow?"

I pat his shoulder politely. "It's probably best you don't."

Not wanting to watch his reaction, I turn around quickly and leave the restaurant, hailing a cab that happens to drive past.

As soon as I'm back in my apartment, I take off my heels and hit dial with a vengeance.

"Hello?"

"You're kidding me, right?"

"What?" Charlie groans. "No good?"

"How about we talk about cheese for an hour?"

"Why?"

"Exactly!"

"I'm so sorry. Gustave seemed like a great guy. When he told me he was a food critic, I thought perfect! You like food, right?"

"I do like food, but what I don't like is being forced to smell cheese and pretend it's just great when really it smells like an asshole."

"How do you even know what an asshole smells like?"

"No more. I can't do this blind date thing anymore. In fact, dating itself is over. I'm happy to be celibate. The end."

"Just calm down, okay?" Charlie sighs. "No one needs to be celibate. It sounds like you've had too much to drink or too much cheese."

I'm about to defend my choice of being celibate when my phone vibrates. Removing the phone from my ear, I quickly glance at the text.

My heart begins to beat fast, excitement running through my veins. Every inch of my body reacts with a desperate thirst, heightened by the currents awakening every part of me. Charlie's voice is lost in the background, and with desperation, I hurry to get her off the phone.

"Charlie, I have to go. I need to be in the office early."

"I'm sorry, Kate."

"It's fine," I rush. "Kiss the girls for me. Bye."

I press 'end call' and re-read the text.

Dominic: *I'll be in Paris next Friday. Shall I book our usual?*

I fall onto the sofa, re-reading his text again before my fingers type on their own accord.

Me: *Our usual will be perfect. See you then.*

Within mere moments, my idea of being celibate has sailed into the night.

Dominic Kennedy is back.

And my body suddenly craves everything I know he'll give me.

Raw, animalistic sex.

No attachments.

No expectations.

The best kind.

THREE

KATE

Four Years Ago

The business card sat between my fingers while I stared at it for the hundredth time that day.

After we left Vivian's birthday party a few nights ago, I made no mention to Eric about my encounter with Dominic. Even if I had said something, I highly doubt he'd have heard since all he could talk about was Thiago. With a gentle reminder, I mentioned Tristan's name to bring him back to reality. Eric tended to focus on the wrong thing at times, especially when he's trying to avoid heartbreak.

"I'm in the prime of my life, Kate. This is as good as I'll ever look," he had cried loudly.

"You're ridiculous. Age can make a man look even sexier. And besides, there's always Botox."

Eric slapped his hand to his chest. "Are you looking at my forehead?"

"No," I dragged, avoiding his eyes. "Stop overreacting. You're missing the point entirely. Love isn't defined by how one looks. You need to have trust in your relationship, or it will never work."

I shook my head to rid myself of the memory. Who was I to give relationship advice? Unless, of course, it's how to be in a relationship with your job. That, I had mastered like a pro. The longest relationship I had was for a year. Even then, I'd barely call it a relationship since he lived in Australia, and I was jetting between the States and London at the time.

Yet something about Dominic piqued my curiosity in ways I hadn't felt in such a long time, if ever. Like a moth to a flame, I'm drawn to the mystery of a man who raised questions even I had asked myself. It's almost as if he climbed into my soul, studied what I had been feeling, and repeated it back word for word.

I want to call him. A part of me is unable to shake the moment which passed between us. But what if I'm so desperate for a moment that I'd worked it up in my imagination. The temptation taunted me like a delicious piece of candy, and unable to resist any longer, I made an executive decision to send him a text.

Me: *Hey, Dominic. It's Kate from last weekend.*
Thanks again for the chat. It was nice meeting you.

The second I hit send, I regretted it instantly. There was absolutely no substance to that text. If I'd gotten a text like that, I'd hit delete faster than you could say *next*.

A shrill echoed through my office, the ring of my phone startled me and caused my body to jump slightly from my chair. Clasping my hand toward my chest to calm my racing heart, I answered the call professionally, noting the private number.

"Kate Hamilton."

"Hello, Kate, I've been waiting for you to contact me," a deep voice greeted, an edge of persistence in his tone.

"Who's this?" I asked, still catching my breath. "Dominic?"

"Yes, the man you texted mere moments ago. I don't bite, you know, you could've called me."

Embarrassed, I closed my eyes, trying to act adult and not give him a cowardly answer. I couldn't understand why I felt somewhat intimidated by a man. Inside the office, I had no problem being a strong, confident woman. I demanded things, and I always got what I wanted.

Straightening my posture, I smiled politely, though he couldn't see me.

"Look, I wasn't sure if you would remember me. Better to be safe than sorry."

"How could I not remember you? A beautiful woman like yourself is simply unforgettable."

There's that word again being thrown around like it didn't affect me whatsoever. I'd been called beautiful many times, but the power he had over me only added to the mystery of it all. Perhaps, I'd been overthinking our encounter. He was a stranger, after all, and one who expressed twice now what he thought of me.

"I'm slightly hurt," he asserted with an air of arrogance. "I was expecting a call sooner."

"Work gets in the way. You know how it is."

"Yes, exactly. Work does get in the way," he stated, pausing only momentarily. "Are you free for drinks tonight?"

I could do drinks. What's the harm in a friendly drink? *Except you want more than just a drink, moron.*

"Sure, I'll come straight from work."

He told me he'd text me the details but gave me some directions. I listened intently, jotting down what he'd said until he said he needed to go.

"Tonight, Kate, I'll be waiting for you."

"See you then, Dominic."

I hung up on the call. My legs were crossed, controlling this desire which flushed through my body with every word he spoke. A gentle knock on my door from my assistant broke my train of thought and brought me back to reality.

All work and no play—my life as I know it.

The bar was located in the meat-packing district. Eric brought me here a few times back when he lived in the city, but I wasn't familiar with the area for the most part. I entered the building, noticing the surroundings being a typical bar with buzzing patrons and music to set the ambiance.

Wooden stools butted up against the brass foot rail caught my attention, as did the back wall with several glass shelves housing every bottle of liquor you could think of. I desperately needed something to calm my growing nerves, so I headed straight to the bar to quench my thirst.

The bartender was quick to serve me, just as fast as downing a gin and tonic in almost under a minute. When I began to feel my limbs loosen, a hand pressed on the small of my back.

Dominic appeared beside me, looking incredibly sexy in a gray blazer with a white collared shirt slightly unbuttoned beneath it. He wore his glasses again, the bane of my existence. How can something so simple be so goddamn sexy?

"You're here," I said, surprised to see him thinking he'd ditch the drinks.

"I'm not one to stand up a stunning woman like yourself."

Dominic motioned for me to take a seat on one of the barstools. As my eyes scanned the area, noticing a few empty tables and chairs in a more intimate spot, I questioned why he wanted to hang at the bar. Loitering at the bar area was where singles generally hang out, hoping to strike up a conversation with someone else or quickly get away if the date wasn't going as planned.

"Nice bar," I commented, admiring the wood-grain countertop.

"Thank you. I own it."

I turn my head to face him with curiosity. "You own this bar?"

Thankfully, I didn't say it was a shit hole.

Actually, it was far from it. It had a certain ambiance, which was relaxing, unlike many of the other places around here. Many patrons were dressed in corporate wear like me, unwinding with drinks after what had probably been a hectic day in the office.

"This, and a few other places."

"Eric never mentioned what you did."

"That's because Eric doesn't know." He motioned for the bartender to serve me another drink before he suggested we take this to a more private area. Thank God, I had started to get a complex of his intentions. "I want to show you something."

We walked upstairs, and taking my hand, he entered a code on a security panel just outside the door. My heart was beating fast, about to fall out of my chest and ready to go into cardiac arrest on the floor. I had no idea why, as this wasn't my first rodeo with a man.

The room was dark, only a glimmer of light coming from a large window. Oddly so, the window didn't appear to be facing outside, and from where I stood, it looked like it had a view of another room.

Dominic stopped me in my tracks, quickly standing before me and blocked my vision toward the window.

"I want you to relax, take it in, and don't think about anything else."

My nerves mix in with confusion. Was he going to fuck me in this room? A part of me was scared. I'd never done anything like this with someone I barely knew. But my body betrayed me, the sensations swam freely and clouded any rational judgment I should have had at that moment.

"I don't understand?" I stuttered, staring into his eyes.

"Do you trust me?"

I hardly knew him, let alone be able to trust him. Yet he's Eric's brother, and surely, our ties should cement the fact that he wasn't taking me to a dungeon to kidnap me.

"I trust you," I repeated, lowering my voice.

He moved behind me and motioned for me to step closer to the window. With every step forward, my eyes widened until the view of the room beneath us consumed my vision.

Men and women filled the room, some old and some young. Some wore clothes, and many were completely exposed. The more I stared below, the more it began to sink in. It must have been a sex club of some sort, given many people were in compromising positions.

My eyes were drawn to a woman on all fours, sucking a man off while two men behind her take turns entering her.

Beside them, an older couple were fucking on their own, completely naked as people circled them and watched.

"A sex club," I mouthed, trying to gather my thoughts. "This is a sex club."

"It's a place for people to let go of their inhibitions."

"Do you—"

"No," he stated firmly.

"Wait, so you just watch from here?"

"Occasionally, but not often."

"I don't understand?"

"I manage the business. I connect important people with people willing to fulfill their needs. See, much like yourself, people don't have time for relationships, but it doesn't mean their sexual desires aren't important. I've created a place where people can express themselves, explore their desires, and walk away without the complication of being tied down to one person."

I tried to process it all but kept coming up with questions. I watched behind the window, and perhaps with Dominic standing so close to me, my body began to betray me. But then my mind shifted to Eric. He had mentioned these places as a joke. He'd have a heart attack knowing his brother was involved in such a business.

Dominic moved closer, trapping me before the glass. Yet he didn't touch me, nor make a move, and his body being inches away ignited a flame which had long been burning down to almost nothing.

"Does it scare you?"

"Yes," I whispered, barely holding my breath. "I don't know. I'm not sure what it makes me feel."

"Just watch."

There was nothing to do but watch. Two women were in a scissor position. Again, there was a small crowd surrounding them while they continued to move. A young man was standing against a wall, two mature women on their knees as they took turns giving him a blow job. My eyes diverted around the room, all the while trying to ignore the pulsating throb between my thighs.

"So, you don't have sex down there with people?"

"No."

"Never?"

"Never," he repeated.

"So, if we dated, what does that mean?"

A small pocket of air gushed behind as he pulled away, forcing me to turn around. Dominic created distance between us as if he couldn't stand to be near me anymore.

"Perhaps I didn't make myself clear, Kate. I don't date. I don't have relationships. This is who I am. I don't mix business with pleasure."

Touching the base of my neck, I narrowed my gaze on him. "So why did you bring me here?"

"Because I could see it in your eyes. Your desire to have a man touch you intimately."

"I'm sorry, I don't understand?" I interjected, crossing my arms in defiance. "You don't want to touch me?"

"It's not my job to touch you. I'm here to open your eyes to another world. A world where every fantasy can be met."

I turned back around to avoid the humiliation which had crept in slowly and gazed at the scene before me. Dominic was proposing I fulfill my desires with a stranger, let go of my inhibitions as well as my morals for the sake of what? An orgasm that lasts not even a minute.

The nerve of him.

Suddenly, a burst of anger rattled me. The air in the room became stifling hot, my blazer had become too tight as sweat started to build beneath my blouse.

"I need... I need to get out of here."

I turn to exit the room before Dominic latched onto my arm, holding me still.

"You'll be back. Everyone always comes back," he stated confidently. "You can play your morals in your head on repeat, but deep down inside, you can't ignore your first initial reaction. Curiosity is the feeder of desire. And with desire becomes your ability to let it all go. You'll see Kate, I promise."

Dominic released his grip, and in a flash, I exited the room with my dignity.

There's no chance in hell I'd succumb to his prediction.

And especially no chance of returning here again.

Dominic may have been sexy, and yes, I'd fantasized about him a lot since I first met him, but those preliminary thoughts didn't consume me whole. I wasn't in that deep, not enough to force me under a current with no chance of survival.

I was still able to swim.

Away from the chaos and away from the man marked as dangerous.

FOUR

KATE

Present

"And so, then he says, what about kids one day?"

Eric's high-pitched squeal causes me to distance the phone from my ear. With my thoughts focused elsewhere, I think of a reasonable response to calm him down.

"So, he's thinking about kids? It's not going to happen tomorrow," I reassure him while scanning the area of the hotel lobby. "Tristan loves you. Don't panic over something that isn't worth panicking about now. You guys just got back together after a long time apart. Slow down and try to enjoy each other's company."

"That's the problem. I'd love to slow down, but Tristan wants to move forward. He's talking about commitment."

When it comes to relationships, Eric dreads the 'C' word. In ways, I don't blame him. Not that I'll openly admit that. Just because it works for some people doesn't necessarily mean it works for others. I believe we should all set our own rules in life, and conforming to society can only set you up for failure. Different people, different rules, and different relationships.

"Eric," I repeat, willing to calm him down with my soft tone. "You love him, right? Just follow your gut."

"My gut has gained ten pounds thanks to his cooking!" Eric's shrill is enough for me to end our conversation. "I'll be the laughing stock of Weight Watchers come fall."

"Stop being dramatic. I have to go," I tell him, noting the time on the clock on the wall above the concierge desk. "We'll talk later."

"You can't go! And anyway, what are you doing? You're so secretive these days that for all I know, you've joined the Parisian mafia and work undercover as some mob boss."

"You've watched *The Godfather* way too many times," I point out to him. "I have some urgent business to take care of tonight. We'll talk later."

I press 'end call' before he has a chance to say goodbye or quote lines from the movie with his terrible impersonation of Marlon Brando.

Keeping my phone in my hand, I scan the hotel lobby area with a flutter of anticipation in my stomach. A few guests wait patiently to be served by the hotel staff with suitcases beside them, waiting to check-in. Many of the guests are traveling couples looking far from exuberant. Their withered faces appear tired from their travels and accompanied with evident jet lag.

Dressed in my beige coat, which looks rather suspicious in this summer heat, I wore nothing but my newly purchased La Perla black corset beneath it. The fabric of my coat against my bare skin heightens the desire desperate to be fulfilled, causing me to bite my bottom lip to control the urges in this public space.

My Jimmy Choo heels click against the marble tiles

while I circle the area like a lost puppy. Rechecking my phone, the screen is crowded with notifications but none of which I need at this moment, including many from Eric with Godfather memes.

I continue to wait for Dominic's text informing me of his room number and attempt to distract myself with the surroundings. Dominic purposely chooses this hotel each time he visits, wanting a tastefully luxurious boutique hotel that still feels intimate, unlike the bigger hotel chains known for their high-occupancy rate and, therefore, people everywhere.

The hotel is located in the heart of Saint-Germain des Prés and just a short stroll to Notre Dame. It's a popular choice amongst adults traveling without children, boasting contemporary-styled rooms with a private terrace. I've grown fond of the place, but perhaps it's the memories attached—the secret rendezvous which occurs twice a year whenever Dominic visits Paris.

Behind the closed door, another side of me emerges. No one to judge me for my lifestyle, the way I allow my body to succumb to the one man who I purposely ran from years ago. Just the thought of it sends a warmth throughout me, teasing me between my thighs while I sit here amongst a crowd of people.

The thrill of our encounters has become an addiction, one so hard to break because as long as the secret remains between us, no one else will get hurt.

It's our rules, our game, and we both win if played right.

Inside my hand, my phone beeps. Glancing down, my eyes wander over the simple text with the number two-one-two. The adrenaline kick starts like an engine ready to roar, and ignoring everyone surrounding me, I make my way to the elevator and up to level two.

When I reach the floor, the room is located in the far west wing. With each step closer, my heart starts to race. My body begins to tingle with an ache only Dominic can conquer. The memory of the touch of his hands against my skin comes to the forefront of my thoughts, making it hard for me to breathe without the slightest of moans.

The door comes closer and closer until I'm standing in front and staring right at it.

Without hesitation, I twist the knob with a hard turn and slowly push the door forward as the dark room engulfs me. Every fiber of my being is vibrating with excitement running through my veins and manipulating my mind to succumb to all its fantasies.

Turning around, I close the door slowly and face it for a brief moment, taking a deep breath to control myself until hands place themselves on my shoulders, sliding my coat off my barely covered skin.

The room is dead silent, all but the sound of his heavy breathing mimicking the hunger of a wolf eyeing its prey. With every exhale, I close my eyes and listen to his desires being played out through these delectable sounds.

Beneath the coat, the new corset is half leather, half lace. The black fabric barely covers my erect nipples caused by a sweep of cold air from the air conditioning, hardening them to a delicious ache.

Slowly, he presses me against the door, his usual greeting, which I've grown to crave. Resting the tip of his index finger on my cheek, he gently glides it down past my cheekbone and the sensitive part of my neck. Closing my eyes, I savor each feeling, allowing my senses to completely take over.

He applies more pressure, pressing me against the door while he cups my chin.

"I've been waiting," he whispers into my ear, grazing his teeth along my lobe. "Fantasizing about every single thing I'm going to do to you."

"Show me," I demand, straightening my posture to invite my dominant persona back into our sick and twisted game. "Show me what you want."

Placing his hands on my shoulders, he swiftly turns me around, so our bodies are face to face. His naked torso teases me in the shadows—a perfect chest sculpted from his rigorous workout routine. I ache to run my hands down, graze each ab with the slightest of touch but know he wants it hard and fast for our first fuck.

His knee jerks my thighs opens, and raising my arms to rest against the door, he enters me without warning, causing me to gasp as my breath catches in my throat.

With each thrust, his rigid and controlled body pushes in deeper. Arching my neck, my voice is trapped inside, willing to be hidden the way he likes it. Dominic isn't like any other man I've been with, begging to scream their names while in the throes of passion.

He demands dead silence.

Only the sound of his cock entering my wet arousal echoes in the room. I crave the sound—the louder it gets, the more I become closer to exploding around him.

Pressing his palm against my neck, I lift my gaze toward the ceiling, closing my eyes and allowing the sensations to burst through me like a rampant storm. But I'm teetering on the edge, barely holding on, every inch of me sensitive to his touch, and the darkness from my eyes being shut becomes a burst of light.

I'm coming undone, the warm sensation swelling into a blissful wave crashing into me. My breathing is uneven, and without a moment to calm myself, he removes himself with urgency and pushes me to my knees to suck him off. My lips wrap around the tip of his cock, sucking him clean until there's nothing left but the sound of his heaving pants echoing inside the hotel room.

In silence, we move toward the bed, the same way we've always done, and once again, he demands me to get on all fours for more, but this time, he urges me to instruct him what to do, our roleplaying only adding to the frenzy unleashing between us.

Every step, every motion, he demands my direction like a puppet being guided on strings. I've learned to listen to my body, void myself of any emotions, and experience sex how Dominic has taught me. Just like in his club, we all chase a fantasy, and mine is coming to life with a man who knows exactly what I need.

I dominate the boardroom, and now, I'll dominate the bedroom exactly the way I want it.

But shortly after I demand he lower himself and finish me off with his tongue, my mind goes completely blank as the second burst of lights flashes before my eyes, and the tidal wave soars through me with such intensity.

Lowering my head, my hands begin to shake, threatening my whole body to collapse on the bed. Breathing in and out, I shuffle toward the pillow and turn myself around, falling onto my back while catching my breath.

Dominic joins me, pulling out a cigarette from the bedside table and lighting it a few moments later. The first time he did this, I didn't care for the smell. But smoking in Paris is welcomed, and over time, I've grown accustomed to it.

The two of us lay in silence. My eyes begin to droop from exhaustion, and rightfully so, I allow them a moment's rest to build my stamina and strength for a few more hours of raw sex.

Yet, something is off. My head doesn't want to relax, almost as if it can sense a storm in the horizon warning me to buckle down and prepare myself. I blame the stress, the nonstop hours I have been working, and the insider-trading debacle which has become a greater issue than we first suspected.

Even my normal sleep routine has been interrupted. I struggle of late to fall asleep without sleeping aids or a glass of wine. For the most part, I ignore the warning signs, but in this very moment, something is pressuring me to pay attention.

My eyes spring open, the voices unable to shut down. The room is dark, but a small ray of sunshine peeks through the violet drapes. Suddenly, thirst consumes me. Beside me, I open the water bottle and take a long-winded sip. When I finish, I notice Dominic staring at the ceiling. Much like me, he appears bothered by thoughts. His cigarette has been extinguished beside him, and although it would be right of me to ask if he's okay, I instantly remember our rules.

I fall back onto the pillow, staring at the ceiling until he clears his throat. It was always bound to happen, his ending of our affair due to his marriage, and I'm certain he's about to say just that. I prepared myself for it a long time ago, removed any emotions harbored, and selfishly prioritized my sexual needs. Dominic fits into my life with convenience. I don't have time for a partner, and work will always be my number one priority.

I experience love in various forms, but life without it is perfectly fine. There's no one to demand my attention and no one to worry about beside myself.

It's the way I set my life up, and nothing will change that.

And so, I mentally prepare myself for his final parting—his exit out of our tryst.

"Kate," he begins with a despairing tone while looking down onto the pristine sheets. He crosses his arms with a pensive expression. "Things aren't working with Allegra."

FIVE

KATE

The bombshell explodes in what should've been this idyllic moment.

We spent the last few hours satisfying our own selfish needs in the sanctity of this hotel room. No one knows where we are, what we're doing, and that's how it has been for the last three years.

Whenever Dominic visits Paris, the trips are always short. His sole purpose for traveling was always due to business, leaving very little time for our rendezvous.

Never did I question nor demand more of his time. Dominic is correct in presuming I need sex without the additional strings. It suits my lifestyle, and we made sure from the beginning that boundaries were set and clear.

No one asked for more, and no one got hurt.

Between work, and well, work, I don't have time for a relationship nor commitment. My sexual needs are pretty much satisfied by him, and what goes on in his life isn't of my concern, just as he has no interest in mine.

But now, reality hits our bubble, the threat to burst too dangerous even to consider.

Of course, things aren't working with his wife. He married her under false pretenses. Allegra's father is a very wealthy man, and marrying her made good business sense. He needed capital, so attached to that came strings. Yes, she's beautiful, and between them they make an attractive couple, but looks can be deceiving.

Allegra travels the world with her girlfriends, staying in luxurious hotels while being pampered, spending copious amounts of money on brands and labels from sheer boredom. Their marriage is built on paper agreements, a recipe for disaster, in my opinion. An opinion I've always kept to myself.

Yet now he has the audacity to tell me it isn't working? What the hell am I supposed to say? Of course, it's not working. You're fucking me on the side twice a year.

"I'm sorry." Feeling vulnerable, I distance myself and pull the sheet over my exposed breasts. "Marriage is complicated."

I regret my words immediately. What advice can I give on marriage? It isn't something I desperately need like everyone else. More so, it looks like hard work. And why should being in a relationship with someone be hard work?

I think of excuses to leave the room. Maybe an important business call may suffice.

"I may have an opportunity to visit more often soon," he continues, much to my detriment.

And the aftershock continues, rattling everything we have built between us. A mutual agreement to have sex when he visited, and that was it.

No, I miss you.

No sentiments whatsoever.

Around Dominic, I treat him like a business associate with respect but keep my personal feelings aside. The last time I opened my mouth, I got burned and barely recovered. The lesson learned to take the good and ignore the bad.

He shuffles, so he's sitting completely upright, crossing his arms as if angered by my silence. "You're not saying anything?"

"Dominic, what would you like me to say?"

"I'd like to know what you think about me spending more time in Paris?"

"I think you have a wife back in the States who would probably have a problem with that unless, of course, you end your marriage."

These talks always ruin the moment and burst the so-called bubble I had blown around this forbidden relationship of ours. Beside me, I can see his body tense from the nature of the conversation, although he raised the topic, not me.

"You want me to end my marriage?" he questions, though his harsh tone makes it more of a statement.

I slide up, sitting against the headboard to gain control of my thoughts. "I don't want anything, Dominic. We made a deal. What happens in Paris stays in Paris. I don't ask questions about your life, and you don't ask about mine. We both get what we want, and that's it."

"But what if I want more?"

"You don't know what more is..." I trail off, steering him off uncharted territory, which only leads to one thing —heartbreak.

"I know I want you, like this."

His hands trace my collarbone, and as my eyes begin to close, my heart starts racing preparing myself for what he's about to do. With Dominic, our relationship is purely physical. He satisfies me in ways no man has ever done. From the very first moment I met him, I knew I was attracted to him, but I didn't realize how deadly that attraction could be and how it changed me in ways I never imagined.

Dominic made his intentions clear from the beginning, and he knew exactly what I needed.

Sex, no attachments, the whole reason for why he's a successful entrepreneur. He knows exactly how to give people what they never knew they wanted.

And I'm no different. I want to give in to my desires, but now he wants more.

The four-letter word destined for trouble.

I sit on the edge of the bed, fastening the ankle strap on my heels. My muscles are tender and sore—hours spent on this bed being devoured by a man who just mentioned leaving his wife. All of which becomes a distant memory overshadowed by multiple orgasms.

"Kate, can we talk some more about this?"

From a man who hardly converses unless it's about a sexual act, this sudden need to open up this closed channel between us comes as quite a surprise but not a pleasant one at that.

Things are fine this way, I want to tell him.

Four years ago, I wanted more—a relationship.

The attachment had consumed me and became a problem, landing me in more trouble than I ever dreamed of—the ill-fated threesome in his club, to the pregnancy scare. I had what felt like zero control over my life. All of which I'd rather forget ever happened.

And from the very first night when he showed me his secret hidden life, he claims to have known exactly what I needed, and he was right. I enjoy my work. I want sex, and being unattached gives me the freedom to live my life how I please.

I don't need more.

Standing, I place the coat over my shoulders, running my arms into the sleeves while he sits up in bed observing me with a persistent gaze. His perfectly sculpted torso is exposed, making it hard for me to concentrate or resist the temptation to climb back into bed with him.

"Dominic, we agreed on nothing more," I forcefully remind him.

I quickly check the time on my phone, noting I only have two hours to dash home, shower, and change before meeting with a client even though it's Saturday. "I have to be somewhere."

Searching on the nightstand, I make sure I have my purse and didn't leave anything behind before he shifts off the bed and stands before me, completely naked. Taking a deep breath, I try to ignore how he towers over me, staring into my eyes like I'm the prey to his hunger. I dare not look below, knowing full well he's erect and ready to retake me to prove a point.

"I have to go. I can't be late for this meeting," I reiterate while trying to keep my hands from touching his chest.

Taking a step back to leave the room, he shuffles quickly and latches onto my wrist before pulling me into him for a deep kiss. His tongue is forceful and steeped in passion, igniting the flame within me I have tried to control. But this time, it feels different. Perhaps, it's the exact same kiss as always. Only now, my emotions are torn between his need to become more intimate and the possibility of what we could be because he wants out of his marriage.

The thought alone terrifies me, giving myself to him

completely. The scar still remains, though hidden in the shadows and never truly leaving me.

Pulling away, I catch my breath before pushing him back. "I'll call you later."

I don't look into his eyes nor turn back as I move closer to the exit. When I finally shut the door behind me, I take a deep breath to gain some composure.

Dominic is a mastermind when it comes to women. Perhaps, this is a game he plays while bored in his marriage. I'm not about to lose nor risk everything I have worked hard for.

I have to control my thoughts, not allow them to wander to a place that should never exist.

He may have rolled the dice, enticed me to play, but I'll be damned if I get hurt in the process. There's only one thing to do, despite my reluctance to do so.

The affair must end.

And I'll make damn well sure it happens tonight.

SIX

KATE

The last remnants of my double-shot espresso go down too smoothly.

"Mr. Auvray," I assert, sliding the thick document across the table to him. "You'll see in our proposal the capital we'll allocate and our forecasted financial return. Jacque, our business manager, had many questions upon his visit last month. Of course, I'd personally like to tour the property and see how Auvray Le Champagne operates."

Reaching out, Mr. Auvray opens the proposal, scanning the papers behind his tortoiseshell glasses. I try my best to ignore his interesting choice in fashion, noting his jacket has leather patches in the elbows.

"Eh, uh, Mr. Edwards," he mentions in his thick French accent. "He will be visiting Paris, *Oui?*"

"*Oui.*" I smile reassuringly. "He'll be arriving on Friday and will be visiting for four days. He will be attending the Versailles Masquerade Ball along with his wife."

"Ah, yes," he offers with a grin. "*Et vous?*"

"Yes, I'll be there, too."

We talk more about the proposal, but judging by his

body language, it's a done deal. Mr. Auvray owns several wineries and needs an investor, or else he can say goodbye to his family's treasure. A few months back when I discussed this with Lex during one of our conference calls, he was keen to expand our business in the winery division. There'll always be a demand for French champagne, and the market trends have proven just that over the last few years.

"Perhaps yourself, along with Mr. Edwards and his wife, will come to stay in my chateau and experience what we have to offer?"

"That's very generous of you, Mr. Auvray. I'll speak to Mr. Edwards and confirm tomorrow?"

Knowing Charlie, anything not involving kids, and she's there in a heartbeat. Though not wanting to assume Lex will be free, I take the cautious side and make a note to ask him later tonight.

We say goodbye with plans to discuss further when Lex arrives.

It's Saturday night in Paris, and the streets are buzzing with people everywhere. Many are walking in groups, quite possibly on the way to attend the ever-so-entertaining Parisian nightlife. Restaurants are crowded, several people dining with laughter escaping the circle they sit amongst.

I smile to myself, yet beneath the smile, exhaustion creeps in like a thief in the night. With every step I take, the ache of my joints comes to fruition, a reminder of the earlier rendezvous with Dominic.

My eyes fall lazily upon the local market on the corner of my street. Entering the store, I pick up a few essentials, including some fresh fruit and a bunch of yellow roses for home. The store attendant tries to flirt with me in French again, something he does on every visit. I grin and nod, not wanting to offend him yet acknowledging that he's young enough to be my son.

With each step closer to my apartment, my feet seem to drag. The royal blue door with the golden doorknob in front of me brings relief, my arms almost turning to jelly from balancing the items purchased at the store.

The familiar scent instantly greets me—strawberry and watermelon from a wax melt I purchased at a market stall a few months back. The silence is welcoming, clearing my scattered thoughts, if only for a short time.

The moment I laid eyes on this apartment, I knew I had to have it. It was during a casual stroll one Sunday when the building caught my attention. The apartment is located on the upper floor in a mid-1920's building with an exceptional open view of the Eiffel Tower, the Seine, and Pont d'Alma—the very reason it became an emotional purchase.

Living in a rental, my plan has always been to acquire real estate since I love Paris so much. The apartment is spacious with south-facing living and reception rooms opening onto a balcony with a spectacular view. The kitchen is fully functional, not that I'm one to spend hours in there since I eat out most of the time.

Then, there's the master suite, generously proportioned with a large walk-in closet and bathroom fit for a queen.

The apartment was a blank canvas, making it all the more appealing. I'd sold one of my units in London, yet still holding onto one in case I ever decide to go back. Between stocks I sold at a hefty profit and my generous executive salary, including bonuses Lex awards me based on company performance, money is something I don't have to worry about, and this apartment soon became all mine.

I finished furnishing it all plus decorating it to my taste.

All in all, it has become my sanctuary and a beautiful one at that.

After putting away the items bought, I draw a bath with candles surrounding me and hit shuffle on my music. Sliding into the tub, the hot water is heaven-sent against my aching muscles. I sprinkle some salts and add a luxurious bath product given to me as a Christmas gift last year from a client of ours.

As my body relaxes, my eyelids begin to close—the thoughts consuming me earlier become a distant memory. The sounds of John Legend play softly in the confined space. There's always something about his voice that evokes emotion or teleports me to a time in my life when my heart conquered, and parts of me were caught up in the tidal wave of being infatuated with a man.

I see Dominic lying on the bed beside me, his weighted gaze etched with desire. The caress of his hands against my skin ignites passion only he can awake within me. When we're alone, nothing is off-limits.

And I'd be a fool to ignore that his words do not affect me.

Long ago, I fantasized about us being more than what we are, but fantasies are just that. Sometimes, we're fortunate, and they come to life. Other times, they bring heartache and more pain than we'd ever care to admit.

I allow myself a moment to wonder, imagining Dominic as more than just a lover. Yet something blocks the daydream, something unknown which doesn't make sense to me.

My eyes spring open, steam clouding my vision. Taking a deep breath, I immerse myself in the water and rid myself of the guilt. How dare he make me feel anything but what I should feel.

I climb out of the bath in a huff, annoyed at myself for overthinking this. Grabbing my silk pajamas, I place them on and plop myself on the sofa with my laptop open.

The familiar ping is continuous, email after email, all needing my attention. Work has always been my solace, and this time will be no different. Time begins to pass, my head starts to clear, and when I begin to feel somewhat better with my thoughts, I switch on the television and start binge-watching *Ghost Hunters*—the perfect distraction on this lazy Saturday night.

Somewhere during an episode of a haunted place in Scotland, my phone begins to ring, causing me to jump with fear. Taking a deep breath, my heart rate runs a million miles as I lift the phone to see Dominic flashing on the screen.

"Hello," I answer relatively short. "Bored in Paris already?"

"Can we talk now?"

Squeezing my eyes shut momentarily, I release them with a sigh. "If we must."

"It's not working out."

"I know, I heard you."

"Well, you must have thoughts?"

"Of course, I have thoughts. But it doesn't matter what I think," I tell him, my voice slightly raised. "This is your marriage. Make your decision based on what you want."

Silence falls between us, forcing me to check my phone to see if the call is still connected.

"I want what we have," he murmurs. "I don't want that to change."

"Things will have to change one day whether you like it or not, Dominic," I remind him, frustrated.

"Why... why would they have to change?"

"Well, for starters, affairs like ours never work long term. Sooner or later, Allegra will catch on." The truth is finally out, and perhaps this may be the straw to finally break the camel's back. "And, what if I meet someone and want a relationship? It wouldn't be fair for us to continue with another man involved."

"Is there another man involved?" he questions rudely, raising his tone.

"There isn't. Not that it's any of your business."

"It is my business," he grates.

"Um... how so?" I sit up, straightening my posture while crossing my arms in frustration. "We agreed to keep our lives separate. We agreed to have sex when you visited Paris. That's all. Don't expect anything more than what we agreed to."

"This isn't a business deal, Kate."

Anger ripples through me as I bite my lip, trying to restrain my thoughts. The sheer nerve of him to throw careless words around and cloud our agreement.

"We had an agreement," I repeat, more so for me than him. "This is what we both wanted."

"Kate..." He gasps, his tone is raspy and barely in control. "I think about us, just so you know."

My breathing stills, while I stare directly at the wall in a catatonic state. His words can be interpreted in so many ways, and being a woman, I know we have the habit of spinning things bigger in our head than what we really think it is. I didn't know how to answer him, not wanting to get my heart involved since I purposely left it out of this equation.

But why now, I want to ask.

Why, after four years, has he finally posed the question I so desperately wanted back then?

"I think about you visiting Paris, too," is all I can say in return, praying he means the same.

"No, Kate," he whispers down the line. "I think about us. You and me... together. A life together, just us."

It was the admission I never expected to come from Dominic Kennedy. I'm left confused and angry, wondering why I'm forced to have to endure this again. Dominic has no understanding of what it's like to be in a committed relationship. He takes from people what he needs. He's made himself into a successful entrepreneur by promoting the exact opposite of commitment. I'm not stupid, knowing all along that this will have to end one day. I just didn't expect it to end like this.

And I refuse to let him change the rules of our game.

"I can't discuss this any longer," I rush, shaking my head. "I think it's best that we don't see each other in Paris anymore."

Drawing a deep breath, I expect him to agree. After all, he can get pussy anywhere he wants. I wouldn't put it past him if he has other women besides myself and Allegra.

"You can run, Kate. But I know you'll be back," he assures, a sadistic edge in his voice. "I'll be traveling to Milan for the week, then back next Monday. Same place, same time."

With his assumption lingering in my thoughts and delaying any response from me, the call ends, and suddenly —he's gone.

Pulling my knees toward my chest, I stare blankly at the television screen while trying to process what happened. The more it plays inside my head, the larger the vicious cycle swirls, and the only thing transpiring is his expectation of me being back in that room.

The sound of a text message comes through with his

name. It's a video file. I hit play and watch the small clip of me being on my knees while I take him all in, sucking every inch of his cock as he films me. I remember the moment, consenting to him doing so.

Another text message follows.

Dominic: *It's in your eyes. You can never escape how I make you feel.*

I hate his observation, the way he makes me believe I have no control whatsoever. My finger swipes away from the message, refusing to respond to him and encourage his behavior. If I have a weakness, he knows exactly what it is before I even can admit it.

My phone rings again, but this time, Charlie's name flashes on the screen.

"Charlie," I greet, trying to sound upbeat before she picks up on my negativity and questions me. Charlie is intuitive, and given she's a lawyer, it's hard to hide anything from her since she has tactics to extract information when she needs it.

"We're all set for arriving on Friday. I'm so excited," she screeches over the phone. "Mainly because I'm kid-free for four days."

"I'm sure you'll miss them."

"Yeah, until I'm asleep in business class on expensive champagne and decadent food, which doesn't involve animal crackers."

"I'll let you guys get settled on Friday, then we'll get ready in your suite before driving to Versailles."

"Lex, um... he won't be driving over with us. He has something he has to do."

"Meeting?" I question, knowing his itinerary and when he plans to visit the office.

"I don't believe so. Drinks with someone," she answers vaguely. "But how much fun is this weekend going to be? Marie Antoinette costumes. Such a fairy tale!"

Charlie's love of romance is rather sickening at times. She's a hopeless romantic, and I'm sure she'll spend all weekend trying to convert me.

"Lucky you're bringing your prince." I laugh.

"Speak of princes—"

I cut her off. "No, no, and no. I'll not go on another one of your dates. I'm going to this alone. There's nothing wrong with that. Embrace singlehood."

"But how about just a date? Nothing serious?"

"No," I state firmly. "This isn't entirely a social event. There's some business I need to tie up."

"I knew it," Charlie almost shouts. "Lex swore I'd have his full attention and no work involved. I swear that man is lucky he's so damn good-looking."

My laughter ripples through the room. "I miss you. It feels like I haven't seen you in forever, but let me tell you about the fabulous chateau we're visiting on Sunday."

"Oh... do tell me more about this chateau," Charlie ooh's over the speaker. "Je suis prêt à tomber amoureux."

"You're ready to fall in love?" I repeat with a smile. "Me, too, Charlie... me, too."

SEVEN

KATE

I can't recall the last time I've been this eager to attend a social event.

Corporate events are more my niche, a chance to mingle with prestige clients in luxurious venues with over-priced champagne and caviar served to the masses. More often than not, invitations to expensive yachts, or even private chateaus, are offered to educate me on Europe's finest markets. A hard offer to refuse unless, of course, a string is attached like some arrogant billionaire looking for a quick fuck.

I never mix business with pleasure. It's a cardinal rule of mine. Being a female in a dominant male industry pushes me to set boundaries. I may be single, but that doesn't give men the right to proposition me, especially when business is involved.

And European men are a different species to the Americans. They are very forthcoming with their intentions and quick to admire beauty when they see it. I'm not immune to the accents either though, during my time spent here, I've managed not to allow it to sway me into compromising positions.

Tonight, I plan to simply unwind and enjoy the festivities. It has been on my bucket list to attend the Grand Masquerade Ball in Versailles for as long as I can remember, but I promised Charlie years ago I'd do it with her since she absolutely loves Marie Antoinette. Between having babies and her busy workload, this is the first opportunity for her to get away for a few days without the girls.

Lex has chosen for them to stay at the Four Seasons, the penthouse suite with a view of the Eiffel Tower from the terrace. It isn't the first time I've been privy to see this suite, having seen it many years ago when I worked as Lex's executive assistant. Since money has never been an issue, Lex only chooses to stay at the finest of hotels across the world.

Inside the lavish space, a hairstylist and makeup artist are fussing over the two of us as we both sit in chairs positioned in front of a large mirror.

"I still can't believe Lex agreed to attend," I mention while trying to keep my eyes closed as eye shadow is applied. "And to wear a costume."

"And not just any costume." Charlie giggles, apologizing as the stylist almost drops the brush. "I had to compromise. His costume is all black with minimal ruffle. Adriana made sure it stayed true to the eighteenth century, but you really should've been there for the fitting. I don't think I have laughed that hard ever. Almost peed my pants and Noa—"

I open my eyes, waiting for Charlie to continue before she clears her throat.

"So anyway... Eric is dying of jealousy. Be grateful he has his parents' wedding anniversary dinner to attend to in

Manhattan, or he'd be here dressed as some desperate gay prince looking to score with a wealthy king."

My mind questions why Eric was summoned to attend his parents' soiree since Dominic won't be in attendance. I try to ignore the countless questions running through my mind and rid myself of thinking anymore about Dominic. Considering our agreement was simple, it's taken a complicated turn and created more stress than necessary.

Just breathe and forget he exists, if only for tonight.

"So, I'm thinking," Charlie concludes with an impish grin. "We take fabulous pictures and post them on Insta. Eric will be foaming at the mouth, which serves him right."

"Poor lil' bugger." I frown, holding back my laugh.

"Oh, so your British slang is back?" Laughter escapes Charlie as I throw a macadamia nut at her from the bowl in front of me. "Besides, it's payback for him dragging me to the most boring art exhibition last week. He claimed he wanted to spruce up his condo with some new art but turns out an ex-lover of his married the artist. The annoying pest just wanted me to rate who would've made a better husband. Him or the upcoming artist."

"You know, I welcome the distance from Eric at times. Aside from Miss Drama Queen, how is everyone else?"

"Good, I guess. Adriana is busy with Andy and Luna along with her fashion line and all their charity work," Charlotte informs with a gleam in her expression. "They just returned from the Philippines."

"Holiday?"

"Not exactly. Julian is writing a new book and needed to do some research. While they were there, they visited some orphanages and, well, you know them. They've spoken to Andrew and scheduled another visit in a few months."

"Oh," I say out loud. "Expanding the family again?"

"No, at least, I don't think so. Just trying to do their part and help those in need." Charlie takes a sip of champagne before continuing, "I wouldn't put it past them, though. Julian is great with Andy and Luna. Adriana has dropped hints a few times, so you never know."

"And things with Lex and Julian?" I ask with a knowing smirk. "Still okay?"

"As okay as it can be." Charlie snorts behind her glass. "They're civil to each other. They can be in the same room and have a healthy discussion on foreign affairs, but I won't exactly call it perfect. For instance, I went over to visit Adriana for coffee, and she was running late. Naturally, I sat with Julian and talked while we waited. Let's just say that my dear husband wasn't so pleased."

"Wait, by any chance, was this about a week or so ago?"

"How did you know?" Charlie raises her brow. "Did he tell you?"

"No, but we had a challenging video meeting with a client. Lex was pushed hard, and you know him, question his ethics, and he'll lose his cool. It put him in a foul mood all day. I'm just saying it may not have been entirely your fault."

"Explains the outburst," Charlie drags, less than pleased. "Honestly, I still don't know how you work with him. The man can be so—"

The sound of Lex clearing his throat prompts Charlie to stop talking. Keeping my smile hidden, I wait with anticipation for the argument to unfold. Standing against the door frame, Lex folds his arms, deliberately raising his brow with a smirk playing on his lips. He's dressed casually for once—a pair of dark jeans and a light blue polo shirt.

I've been caught in the crossfire during many of their

arguments, including the infamous fight in the restaurant when I first discovered Charlie was the woman Lex had been hopelessly in love with. Over time, it no longer bothered me. Just like when two of your siblings are fighting, and you're in the corner with a tub of popcorn, glad it isn't you for once.

"Don't look at me that way," Charlie warns him with squinting eyes. "You know you can be a pain in the ass. If I had to work with you, I'd have filed a complaint to Human Resources on day one."

"Remind me why I married you again?" he questions, rubbing his chin.

"I'm great in bed. I can cook, plus you knocked me up, so..." Charlie answers confidently, grinning at her reflection as Lex remains unusually quiet. "Don't you have somewhere to be? Drinks with your friend?"

An odd glance passes between them, prompting me to pay closer attention. Lex isn't the type of person to keep 'friends.' For as long as I've known him, his ruthless persona landed him enemies more than anything. Most of the so-called friendships he has are all because of Charlie.

"Yes," he agrees, checking his phone. "I'll be back soon to change and will meet you both in Versailles."

"We can wait," I offer, watching him closely. "I'm sure we can be a little late."

"I'd rather you ladies don't miss anything." He moves toward Charlie, kissing her on the cheek as something passes between them. Surprisingly, Charlie doesn't argue with him and tells him to enjoy drinks.

The moment he leaves, I ask the questions lingering at the tip of my tongue.

"What was that about?"

"What are you talking about?"

"Lex rarely goes out with friends. Who's this person he's meeting?"

"Some guy he knows." Charlie brushes it off like it's not a big deal. "Look, it's probably business since everything always is. As you know, his interest has shifted to the European market, so I don't expect to be spending quality time with him here, which is why I have you."

Breaking into a genuine smile, I ignore my curiosity and change the subject, asking her about the girls. When it comes to talking about her daughters, Charlie can go on for hours. I miss all three girls, and last time I saw them was a year ago when I had a two-day conference in Manhattan. Charlie flew over with them so we could spend a little time together. There's no doubt she has her hands full, another reason why children are great to spoil but equally lovely to hand back at the end of the day.

The makeup artist and hairstylist finish working on us, prompting me to put my costume on. With the help of the two of them, I step inside the dress as they button the back one by one. The Marie Antoinette-inspired dress is deep red with heavy black brocade, trimmed with gold pearls and diamantes. The dress is buttoned, ultimately making my breasts look enormous in the square-cut neckline. Considering I am not wearing a bra, the firm and sheer size of them leaves me speechless.

"Kate," Charlie mouths with her eyes wide. "You look amazing! Plus, your boobs... you're so going to get some with a rack like that."

"Get some by a man wearing questionable tights?" I laugh, clasping the back of my choker. "I need to be really drunk for that to happen."

"You never know." Charlie nods with a grin. "Tonight could be your night."

"I'm not interested in meeting anyone. As long as we have fun, that's all that matters. Don't leave me hanging and run off for a quicky in the hotel room."

This moment could've been an opener for mentioning Dominic. Yet, over the years, I chose to keep our encounters to myself, knowing exactly how Charlie feels about him. As expected from a best friend, she only wants the best for me and reminds me of my worth every time we speak. Charlie is very vocal about Dominic's lifestyle, which is why I choose again to ignore my thoughts and keep quiet on the matter.

"Honestly, Kate, you're the female version of Lex. All work, no play. I understand the importance of sacrificing a personal life to fulfill your ambitious goals, but when are you going to start putting yourself as number one?" Charlie rambles, her deep stare garnering some sort of response.

"I'm fine the way things are," I answer confidently. "Let's just enjoy tonight, please."

The large mirror gives me ample space to inspect my entire ensemble.

Charlie busies herself by putting on her dress. Adriana designed her an emerald-green gown with a black-lace mask. The color itself is breathtaking.

Placing my black mask on which is made from delicate lace, I take a moment to admire my completed outfit. My hair sits softly to the side, pinned with curls to match the era. I colored it only recently to an ash blonde, somewhat liking this shade from my natural tones. Unlike many of the other images I have seen online when preparing for this event, I opted not to wear a wig as did Charlie. Between the summer heat and the heavy dress we'll have to wear all night, a wig was deemed annoying and unnecessary.

Charlie turns around, fully dressed as her eyes sparkle

with excitement. She's also drunk at least two glasses of champagne while we've sat here, and I expect her to be completely drunk by midnight at best. I don't mind. Drunk Charlie is fun Charlie. There's always that one friend who makes it ten times more fun when they're drunk, and Charlie takes the medal with Rocky coming in a close second.

"Adriana is brilliant," she gushes with a fake British accent causing me to erupt into laughter. "This dress is absolutely perfect."

"Are you ready to party and drink expensive French champagne in Versailles?" I cheer, holding my glass to clink with hers. "La vie est belle!"

The two of us drink while we sing along to "Celebration" by Kool & the Gang.

"Life is beautiful," Charlie repeats in English. "And tonight will be the night I've been waiting for."

We arrive just before the night fountain show, passing time by strolling the beautiful gardens during twilight. The ball itself doesn't begin until eleven thirty and typically finishes just before dawn.

There's a flurry of excitement from those attending, dressed impeccably in their costumes and congregating in groups to take several pictures to mark the occasion. Tourists also occupy the area, admiring the surroundings and taking out their phones to snap photographs of those willing to pose for them.

The sun begins to set, a canvas of beautiful colors adorning the sky. Rich hues of red blended with oranges, purples, and crimsons, all of which bring a sense of calm within me.

"The sky is stunning," Charlie says, wistfully, her thoughts just like mine. "France is beautiful. I understand why you've chosen to stay here."

"It's beautiful," I agree as we both still our movements. "I really can't imagine living anywhere else right now."

Charlie is distracted, glancing at her phone with a knowing grin. "Lex just sent me a very profane text on how uncomfortable it is wearing tights."

"Why am I not surprised?" I muse, smiling at people as they walk past in their costumes. "How long until he arrives?"

"Soon. So, listen, there's something—"

I interrupt Charlie, prompting her to follow the crowds moving toward the large fountains. "Hurry... let's get a good spot. I don't want to miss anything."

Everyone else has the same idea, and with the night's sky fallen upon us, the view is nothing short of spectacular. Unable to hide my smile, I gaze around me, perplexed that France always offers something new which simply takes my breath away.

The night fountain show features water and fire tricks set to music. We stand together, watching and clapping with the rest of the crowd. The sheer timing of it all is impeccable and one they have mastered without any fault.

"There you guys are."

Lex's voice breaks me from my daze. I turn to face him, dropping my eyes toward his feet as I look at his costume. His facial expression says it all, the uncomfortable feeling as he appears to squirm. The outfit he's wearing is black with an emerald green frilly shirt beneath his jacket. The same as

Charlie and me, he opted not to wear a wig but wore a mask to stay in theme.

"Nice tights," I mention teasingly. Charlie warns me with her eyes to shut up until her expression changes, and a nervous smile graces her face. "Charlie, are you okay?"

"Um, so I was trying to tell you earlier that—"

The bang of the fireworks drowns out her words, exploding above us in vivid colors to ignite the otherwise black sky. People ooh and aah, raising their heads to watch the animated show while applauding. According to my online research, the fireworks appearing is the beginning of what's guaranteed to be an unforgettable night.

I'm beyond ready for tonight, desperate to drink champagne, dance away, and forget anything exists besides the excellent company of my close friends. Oh, and a small amount of business I plan to attend to before the liquor deems me incoherent.

A gust of wind sweeps past us, bringing with it a familiar scent. Unwillingly, I freeze on the spot, twitching my nose, trying to pinpoint why this scent is consuming my thoughts and igniting all my senses. It's almost as if it transports me to a time in my past. I have no clue where or when but only remember pleasant moments.

"Kate, are you listening?" Charlie questions.

"Sorry, it was loud. You were saying?"

"I've set you up on another date, but before you say—"

I raise my hand, prompting her to stop. "How many times do I have to tell you, Charlie? After your last disastrous attempt to set me up, what makes you think I would ever try again?"

"I'm slightly offended." The voice chuckles behind me.

The voice, much like the scent, onsets a stream of memories. Memories I buried along with many other things.

With a slow and steady turn, my body shifts to see who belongs to the voice.

My eyes are wide, fixated on the man standing before me. The mask covers a portion of his face, but beneath the black façade lays the eyes of a man I had once loved in more ways than one. The piercing hazel sea of speckles dances in delight as they stare back at me.

Noah Mason.

EIGHT

KATE

The memories are playing like an old-time movie reel.

Each scene brings on a wave of emotions, the same emotions which were buried since the moment I left the States and hopped on a plane to Paris. The familiarity and warmth rush through me like a tepid ocean wave, calming my nerves and comforting me, much to my surprise. But as Noah's stare deepens, the momentary calm is replaced by a tight feeling in my chest and a blank expression I can't seem to shift.

"I heard you needed a date," he simply states.

My head tilts to look behind him as if I expected someone else to be hovering around him. Eric is my first thought, but then, I see no one besides strangers and, of course, Lex and Charlie, brows raised as they wait for my reaction.

I retract slowly, examining the man standing before me. It's been over three years since I last saw him at the hospital. The day I decided to walk away and start a new life. The same day he told me he loved me yet, in the same breath, announced he was about to start a new journey by welcoming a child with Morgan.

That moment was the final puncture to an open wound I'd allowed to be exposed for too long. Undeniably, I miss having him as my best friend, someone I grew fond of and relied upon during our time together. But something never meshed with us. We were great as friends, but nothing more. And no matter how much I tried to ignore the said fact, Noah's admission sealed the deal. He'd fallen in love with another woman, and they were to make a life together.

As for me, I did what I've always done in life, moved on to a new adventure and focused on myself, closing the final chapter on that book.

We remained friends—'friends' being the operative word—via social media, but I rarely logged into my account and never posted anything. Unlike Eric, I didn't find any use in the platform. There are better things to do with my time than aimless scrolling and 'liking' someone's post.

Neither one of us reached out to each other, aside from a message I passed on through Charlie to congratulate him on the birth of his daughter. And so, we drifted apart and haven't spoken since.

Now, he's standing before me, still looking as heart-breakingly handsome as ever.

Noah is dressed similarly to Lex in a black costume, possibly designed by Adriana if the ruffles are anything to go by. On closer inspection, he looks slightly thinner than I remember him but still appears muscular beneath the tights he's wearing.

Though behind the black and gold mask, his face tells a different story. His eyes don't shine as bright as I once remembered, and his cheeks have thinned out—another sign of his weight loss. His normally freshly shaven face is smothered with a thick beard yet manicured and not over-grown like I'd noticed on some men. It adds to his masculinity and somewhat suits him.

"Can a long-lost friend get a hug, or do you prefer I stand here so you can continue to stare at me in silence?" He rubs his beard, a smirk following. "I'll tell you now that I charge a dollar a minute."

I shuffle closer to him, wrapping my arms around his neck. His body is flush with mine as he laces his arms around my waist, bringing me in for a very tight embrace. Closing my eyes, I take a deep breath at the same time my heart begins to weigh heavily. In Noah's embrace, his scent is even more memorable. Slowly, my memories drift to the countless nights I'd rest my head on his shoulder or the few times I would lay my head against his chest and listen to his heartbeat. There was a time when I could memorize it's beat, almost like it played a tune whenever I was around him.

"You're here..." my words fumble out in confusion. "I don't understand?"

Releasing himself from me, he remains a few inches away as my hands fall back to my sides.

"The question-and-answer portion of the date is now paused."

He motions for me to watch the fountains. The water sprays up with lighting surrounding it. The people watch in awe, and all the while, my confusion is firmly at the fore-front of my mind.

Noah leans over, his breath close to a whisper. "I can hear your thoughts. Charlie said you need a date, and I need a drinking buddy."

Just as my mouth begins to open, fireworks shoot into the sky again, the ray of colors starting the grand event in style. Everyone watches with excitement until they finish, followed by the large crowd assembling like a herd toward the main entrance.

"Are we ready to head in?" Charlie asks, biting her bottom lip.

I nod, choosing to keep my opinion on her elaborate stunt to myself. If I cause a scene about the issue, she'll assume it's because I have unrequited feelings toward Noah. Annoyed with her secrecy on his attendance, I opt to pick a better time to discuss this, which will most likely be soon after the champagne has flowed through my veins, giving me the courage to say what I really think.

The four of us walk toward the VIP line, which is moving quicker than the general admission. A few months ago, when Charlie told me she wanted to attend, I spoke to a few colleagues who suggested we purchase the extravagant tickets. It would give us lavish tables to sit at, buffet food, and unlimited drinks.

The selling point being the unlimited drinks.

As we enter the main ballroom after checking in, it's like stepping into a dance party with performing acts. Everywhere you turn, there's something to look at, which momentarily distracts me from Noah grabbing my hand and pulling me along with Lex and Charlie.

Some performers stand on podiums, moving their limbs in what I assume is interpretive dance. Another is doing a juggling act with fireball lanterns, drawing a crowd to watch their amazing skills on show.

Strobe lights dart across the large event space, neon colors against the dark walls in beat with the music which is playing. There's so much to take in, and I begin to understand why people lose themselves for hours amongst the entertainment, which is so much more fun while dressed in a costume.

Lex finds our table and, of course, he pulls some extra strings and makes sure we have the bells and whistles. We're positioned upstairs with the best view of the entire venue, close enough to see the main stage. The table is also near the buffet and bar, plus restrooms.

A bucket of chilled champagne sits in the middle of our table. Without delay, I pop it open and pour myself a glass, drinking it without even releasing a breath. Lex and Noah watch me in amusement, whereas Charlie cocks her head to the side, knowing she's just about to encounter the peak of the storm.

"How about we grab more drinks?" Lex suggests to Charlie.

"You stay, Lex," I almost push him back onto the seat. "I need to have a word with Charlie."

I don't give him a chance to answer, pinching her arm until we're at the bar.

"Ow!" She scowls, yanking her arm away from me. "You're hurting me, Kate!"

"What were you thinking, bringing Noah?" I yell, exasperated.

Still rubbing her arm, she lets out a huff. "I was thinking, wouldn't it be fun?"

"Fun?"

The bartender serves us straight away. I order an expensive bottle of champagne and bourbons for the men. "Charlie, Noah and I are... not really friends anymore."

"Look, Kate. To be honest, Noah needed some time to think, and I thought this would be great. You know my opinion on what happened years ago. He's not in a good place right now, and I'm worried, okay?"

When it comes to Noah's personal life, I told Charlie to refrain from telling me anything. As far as I'm concerned, he and Morgan are starting a family. He loves her, and marriage was imminent. The less I know, the better.

But, of course, Eric opened his big fat mouth to me a few months back during one of his drunken late-night rants. According to him, Noah and Morgan are separated, though he doesn't know the details as to why. I don't pry, nor question Charlie or anyone else. If Noah needs me as a so-called friend, there's ample opportunity to reach out. Despite what happened to us, I'd never push him away if he needed me. However, I don't want to be caught in the crossfire knowing all too well my presence in Noah's life way back when is an issue for Morgan.

The tray of drinks is served, but I pull Charlie to stop before we take it back.

"What's going on?" I finally cave, exhaling before continuing. "Is this serious? Is he sick?"

"It's not my place to share his problems. Just be his friend, Kate. That's all he needs right now.

With every step back toward the table, Charlie's words echo inside my head. Being a 'friend' to Noah is more complicated than I care to admit to her and me. The last time I got attached, the flame reached me in the end and burned me, leaving a prominent scar I'd covered up until tonight.

Charlie slides into her chair, leaning closer to Lex as the two of them kiss. I shift my gaze in the opposite direction before deciding to drink some more. Noah sits in silence, staring at the main arena with a glazed expression. I'm drawn to the way he barely blinks, almost like he's in a catatonic state. Indeed, if he were sick, Charlie would've told me the truth. But then again, what if he's terminally ill? He is looking awfully thin. *Jesus Christ, no, let it be something else.*

"We're going to go dance for a bit," Charlie yells over the music. "You guys want to come?"

I shake my head. "I need to find a client. He's supposed to be here with his wife. I'll join you guys later."

Charlie frowns but only momentarily before Lex pulls her away and out of sight.

I pour myself another glass, desperately wanting to ease the nerves. I have no idea why I'm nervous, but perhaps my heart getting bruised the last time we were close would be a good indication of why I'm on edge.

"So..." I mumble, running my fingers on the edge of the glass.

"So..."

I let out a sigh, unsure how to act around him. So much has changed in our lives, chances are we aren't the same people we were years ago.

The music softens, an intermission, though less disco-like beats still played in the background.

"How's work been?"

"Busy but the same, really," he replies casually. "Not as challenging anymore, and I've found my foot in the publishing industry."

"Good. I know you were concerned about learning the ropes."

"That was three years ago," Noah reminds me.

"Right."

The awkward silence raises its ugly head again. Why did it have to be so damn hard? This is the same man you got arrested with while naked on a beach in Malibu. The two of us sat inside a jail cell waiting for Charlie to bail us out. It wasn't our finest moment. Add to that, he'd seen me at my worst, crying over a man who had treated me like yesterday's trash.

The reminder of Dominic and his desperate pleas come racing to the forefront of my mind. What would Noah think if he knew the truth? The idea itself is ridiculous. There's no reason why Noah should find out. As long as I keep my mouth shut, the secret will be safe with me.

But Noah is the man I once poured my heart and soul out to. He knows me better than I knew myself.

Past tense.

Life has changed.

"And you? Lex tells me you've done amazing things in Europe, plus Charlie says you've had the opportunity to travel a fair bit. Sounds like quite some life."

My eyes widen with surprise. I had no idea Charlie or Lex spoke about me to Noah. Did he ask about me? Or was it said in passing? Calm the fuck down, Kate. You're over analyzing this.

"It has been," is all I say.

Noah diverts his eyes away from me, letting out a breath. "Kate, I'm still the same guy. Maybe a bit broken but still the same guy."

"It's been a while," I remind him, desperate not to get into the semantics of our friendship. "Let's get something to eat."

We make our way to the buffet, which is surprisingly not overly crowded. There's so much food, and yet suddenly, my appetite dwindles. Reminding myself that alcohol and an empty stomach don't mix, I make the conscious decision to eat at least something.

My food palate has adjusted with all the business meet-ings and dinners I've attended over the years. My trick is to drink as much as I can without coming across as a drunk, then eat the food served and never ask what's on the plate. The less known, the better. It turns out snails aren't that terrible and tasty if prepared correctly.

"So, tell me... snails. Yay or nay?" Noah purses his lips, questioning the dishes sitting on the silver platters.

"Considering you eat peppermint ice cream, which is still widely disgusting, maybe a yay for you. It's rather enjoyable."

"Rather enjoyable?" He raises his eyebrows with a sneer. "The slug which swooshes his mushy body against the ground?"

I motion for the waiter to place two on my plate. Scraping the escargot with my fork, I raise it toward his mouth.

"Do I have to?"

"It's rude not to," I state, keeping my expression straight. "The French are renowned for their excellent cooking skills."

He takes a bite, and while his face is somewhat confused, he manages to chew without spitting it out into a napkin.

"It's not bad."

"Trying something new is a way to explore the world," I offer, taking in all the food before us.

"I wouldn't know." Noah dips his head, staring at his empty plate. "I've been stuck in hell."

And the giant elephant inside the room makes its long-awaited appearance, wearing a pink tutu and performing *Swan Lake*, desperate for our attention. I don't want to invite questions because as long as I don't know about his personal life, then he shouldn't ask questions about mine. But then Charlie's words about him needing friends and her worry over him comes back tenfold.

"Charlie is worried about you."

"The whole world is worried about me," he deadpans, filling his plate quickly, looking desperate to escape the conversation just as much as me.

We sit down with our food, but both of us are barely eating. I've taken a few bites, noticing Noah picking aimlessly. While sitting at the table, my purse vibrates. Sliding my phone out, a text message from Bouvier Fontaine, a client of ours, is unopened on my screen. My eyes scan quickly over the text. Bouvier apologizing for having to postpone our discussion tonight. His father has fallen ill and has been taken to the hospital. I type a response, sending him prayers, then a quick text to my assistant, Emile, to remind me to check-in tomorrow with Bouvier to ensure his father is stable.

"Shit," I mouth loudly.

"What's wrong?"

"Client had something come up. He won't be here, and I'm eager to finalize a deal we've been working on for quite some time."

Noah shakes his head with a smug expression. "All work, no play. Who have you become?"

"I have fun," I answer defensively. "There's nothing wrong with attending to business during an event like this. The European market is different from the States. It's about cultivating relationships and investing time into making it a strong union for both sides to come out winning."

"Wise words said," Noah chides. "Although I think it's unfair to judge Americans for not cultivating relationships. Sometimes, you give it your all, your best. You work damn hard, but the other person doesn't share the same vision as you. In the end, it all just falls apart, and you question the decisions you made, which led you to this outcome."

The resentment in his tone lingers along with his words. I'm not quite sure whether we switched to talking about something else, and judging by the bitter expression, it's a fair call to say we have.

"Well, that's why you need to make your position strong from the beginning. Don't let someone else dictate the journey. The best relationships last when two parties are in agreement."

"And sometimes you've done all that, but it's still not enough," he throws back.

"Hey!" I cross my arms with frustration while raising my voice. "I don't know what your problem is, Noah, but it shouldn't be me. We've been around each other for like, what, five minutes, and you've got this chip on your shoulder. I don't have time for your mind games or whatever the hell you're doing. I came here to have fun, so excuse me while I go do exactly that."

I yank the skirt of my dress so as not to trip, scanning the area before deciding to hit the dance floor on my own. Noah's hand grips on my arm, causing me to stiffen.

"I'm sorry, okay? I didn't mean to..." He lets go, running his hand through his hair while pinching his lips together. "You're right. This isn't your battle, so I shouldn't take it out on you."

I'm about to tell him he's right. It's not my battle, so don't include me in his mess until he extends his hand and softens his expression. "Let's go dance."

I follow him to the dance floor but not without our drinks. We dance to music, which isn't as comfortable in our costumes. The more we dance, the more we drink. The more we drink, the more we laugh while the room becoming a hazy sight. Noah leaves to use the restroom, leaving me with Charlie as Lex wants a break.

We dance for what feels like hours. Charlie makes sure to take selfies to send to a jealous Eric. Somewhere during another fit of laughter, Noah and Lex join us once again. We've become friends with a group of girls and formed a small circle. Our bodies sway to the music, champagne spilling from our glasses while trying to drink and dance simultaneously. Arms wrap around my waist, providing me with the comfort I've missed. I don't push Noah away, allowing him to hold onto me as he has done so many times. It pisses off two of the women who are trying to get near him, but what do I care. The room is my oyster or whatever the saying is.

You're drunk. You can't even get the damn saying right.

Tonight has been just what I needed, allowing me to unleash the tension chaining me down the past week. Feeling liberated on copious amounts of champagne, my body sways in tune to "The Hills" by The Weeknd as Noah draws me close to him, our faces only inches apart. I lean in closer, about to whisper in his ear how much I missed him when the devil's eyes find me from across the room.

Dominic.

NINE

KATE

Dominic moves toward where we're standing with Allegra attached to his arm, making quite the dashing couple.

I've only met her once—the first time Dominic introduced her as his fiancée. Despite it being years ago, the face has been etched in my memory—the deep green eyes against her olive skin to her perfectly sculpted features descendent from her Italian heritage. Without a doubt, she's beautiful. And no matter how scorned I was upon first meeting her, I can't ignore my insecurity stemming from the ugly disease of *comparison*.

But that was then, and now, I'm no longer a woman driven by my emotions. No one makes me feel less than what I deserve to be. I control my life and no one, especially her, has the power to change that.

The closer they get, the more their costumes become apparent. Allegra is wearing a century-style satin gown in royal blue with distinctive gold lace trim. Sitting on top of her head is a white wig, styled to the event's era and theme. Dominic is wearing an aristocrat suit, similar to Lex and

Noah, with a simple mask. The shade of royal blue and gold matches Allegra's costume to a tee.

The perfect couple.

Only a few feet away, my breath begins to hitch, and the champagne swooshes in my stomach in an unpleasant way. A wave of nausea climbs up my throat before I purposely swallow and tell myself to get my act together. All these unwanted feelings need to chill the hell out and disappear, if only for the next few moments.

"Lex Edwards," Dominic greets with a polite smile, extending his hand toward Lex. "A pleasure to see you again."

It takes a moment for Lex to realize it is Dominic, shaking his hand before turning toward Charlie.

"This is my wife, Charlotte Edwards."

"Dominic Kennedy," he introduces, his eyes entirely on Charlie and devouring her in a way which Lex appears bothered by. "I've heard a lot about you... from my brother, of course."

When it comes to poker faces, Charlie is a professional. Given her career choice of being a lawyer, which involves arguing for a living, attending court, and never showing the other players your cards, I know her well enough to know she's playing the game right now.

Forcing a smile with the tilt of her head, she extends her hand out politely to shake Dominic's. "All good, I hope, though we met years ago at your mother's Christmas party."

"Right, of course," he answers, then purses his lips, turning swiftly until his complete attention is on me.

The shift of his gaze falls on the floor, trailing up my dress and past my ample bosom where he bites his bottom lip before looking into my eyes. Keeping my expression entirely still, my lips are tight, pretending to be the old friend and not a part-time lover who fucked him a week ago.

He leans forward to kiss both my cheeks in a bold move, something Europeans are known for despite Dominic being American. The graze of his lips against my skin ignites a flame, but I pull away quickly not to draw further attention to us.

"Kate, you've met Allegra," he goads with a knowing smirk on his face. "My wife."

His wife. Arrogant prick for reminding me.

Beside him, Allegra studies me with a piercing stare. "Yes, of course."

Following Dominic, she leans forward to kiss both my cheeks. The guilt consumes me, eating away at my conscience. Allegra is no longer someone in the shadows. She's living and breathing while clutching onto her husband for dear life—a husband who so quickly devotes his time to my body on his business trips to Paris.

The silence between us begins to alarm me. What if she found out? Can she tell right now that something has passed between Dominic and me? In a frantic panic, the scent of Noah catches my attention, causing me to act quickly.

"And this is Noah," I blurt out, resting my hand on Noah's shoulder. "My partner."

The moment 'partner' leaves my mouth, I mentally scold myself for being such an idiot. *The boyfriend* sounds juvenile, and my date is no competition for a wife. Lover seems inappropriate, so what else can I possibly say?

Dominic's expression is perplexed, yet he reaches out to Noah, who reluctantly shakes it.

"Quite some woman you have as your date," Dominic mentions arrogantly.

Noah laces his arm around my waist, bringing me in

closer before he moves my hair away from my neck and kisses it softly. My skin burns at the touch of his lips, but I blame it on the confrontation, crowded room, and the weight of the dress combined with too much champagne.

"The one who got away..." Noah murmurs, lifting his gaze to meet Dominic's, "... but now she's mine."

Charlie's eyes widen with surprise. The champagne she had been drinking almost chokes her, and she makes a gurgling sound while she tries to compose herself.

Dominic's distant stare lacks warmth—the jealousy eating away at him as Noah's touch lingers on me. And Noah plays just as mean, goading him because he has absolutely nothing to lose.

"It was nice meeting all of you." Dominic's tone turns stiff, his glare behind the mask unnerving. "Enjoy your time here. I'll have a few more days in Paris as Allegra visits some friends in Venice. Have a good night."

With a final gaze, his deep stare portrays a thousand words unable to be said between us. The two of them walk away as Allegra slips her hand in his, turning her head for a brief moment to look my way.

Quickly, I shift my focus toward Noah and force a smile, making sure I appear fine and not rattled by what just happened.

"Um... right," Charlie drags, her eyes worried. "Do we need to talk about this, or are you okay?"

"Of course, I'm okay," I lie, raising my lips with assurance. "I haven't seen him in years. Too busy with work, plus I haven't been back to Manhattan."

"The guy's a jerk," Noah grunts, pulling himself away from me.

I turn to face him. "Look, I'm sorry I said you were my

partner, a momentary lapse. I don't know what I was thinking. Just acted in defense."

"He's looking at you like a piece of goddamn meat."

Narrowing my eyes, laughter unwillingly escapes me.
"Like you don't look at women that way? Please, could you
be any more judgmental?"

Dropping his shoulders and ducking his chin, his
sudden change of body language comes as a surprise. "No,
Kate. I don't look at women like that. I was married and
gave my marriage all I could. It wasn't my choice initially to
separate, but sometimes life deals you fucked-up hands. So,
before you think I'm like other men, perhaps understand
why I made certain decisions before assuming I cheated on
my wife, which is why I'm in this fucking mess."

I'm stunned, diverting my attention to Charlie for
answers. She bites her lip, moving closer to Noah to console
him. I can see the fire and rage within him, the anger which
looks targeted at himself. But his admission makes no sense
to me, and before I even have a chance to ask, he's off to the
bar with Lex following him.

"What the hell was that?"

"As I said, Kate, Noah's in a bad place. I was hoping this
trip would give him some breathing space, but maybe..."

"But I don't understand? Why did he mention
cheating?"

"Maybe, for tonight, we just forget. Drink and be
merry," she suggests, releasing a long, low sigh. "Tomorrow
is a new day, and there's time to ask questions. This is a
once-in-a-lifetime opportunity, so let's be present."

Charlie's optimistic 'let's live in the moment' does
nothing to curb my frustration. Sitting back at our table, the
mood becomes somber. I watch Noah from across the room
as he leans on the bar for support. Lex is pushing shot

glasses toward him. It's unlike Lex to make someone else drink their problems away. And although my worry for Noah deepens, I remember how easily he chose Morgan over our friendship.

My drunken state does nothing but dredge up unwanted memories from my past. Wanting a moment to myself to regroup my thoughts while hazy, I tell Charlie I need to use the restroom.

As I walk away toward the restroom, carrying the skirt of my dress in my hands rather than drag the massive piece of fabric along the floor, I turn the corner and see the sign. The closer I get, the more desperate I become to pee, wondering how I'll manage in this gown.

Releasing a breath to control my urges, a hand grips my arm, pulling me into another corridor.

"Who is he?" Dominic's nostrils are flaring like a crazed bull behind the gate, ready to attack. He lets go of my hand and rests it against the wall, purposely blocking my exit. The muscles on his face have tightened, a side to him I have never seen before. If I didn't know better, someone is jealous.

"Noah? He's my fr..." I think about using the word 'friend' but what does it all matter, anyway? Dominic has Allegra, and our personal lives are just that—personal. "Someone very close to me. We go way back."

He runs his hands through his hair recklessly, ruining the perfect style he sported only moments ago. "Is he fucking you?"

His tone is anything but calm—forceful with urgency as his eyes flare with anger like this is a problem. I don't care for the possessive stance, not when my life never posed a question until now. And how dare he be allowed to spew this volatile assumption thinking I'm some sort of whore.

The word is unnerving. It's unforgiving with its meaning when used against us women. Maybe that's who I have become. I didn't seem to care he was married, nor that he could be sleeping with other women. I used him for my own selfish sexual needs, so it paints an incredibly clear picture. I've created a monster and fallen victim as his prey.

"I'm not answering that because it's irrelevant." My tone remains controlled, refusing to feed into his jealous outburst. "What exactly do you want, Dominic? I thought we made the rules very clear."

The corridor is small and dimly lit. There's an emergency exit plus an unmarked door. In the tight area, he paces back and forth with fists clenched beside his thighs.

"I don't like you here with him," he almost spits.

"Excuse me? You don't like me here with *him*?" I repeat, tilting my head. "Where exactly would you like me to be?"

He stops mid-step, the skin bunching around his eyes with a pained stare. "I'm leaving Allegra."

"Dominic, I—"

His body falls flush with mine, pinning me up against the wall with a shallow breath only inches away. My armor stands tall, refusing to let him break me.

Goddammit, why do men have to be such assholes!

"I'll be in Paris on Monday. Please meet me so we can talk."

"About what?" I cry.

"Us."

My hands fall onto his chest to push him away. When he's finally not crowding me, I cross my arms in defiance, ready to go to war. "There is *no us*! Jesus Christ, Dominic. You wanted us to be exactly how you set us up to be. I don't understand why you suddenly want to talk?"

There's the sound of people coming toward us, laughing and giggling, then they disappear into the restroom.

"Monday, please?" He begs with his eyes. "Look, we're both angry right now. No good will come of this."

"I need to get out of here," I mutter, avoiding eye contact with him until he cups my chin and raises it to meet his gaze. His persuasive stare crumbles my tough exterior, the walls falling to pieces with a surge of pain following. "I'm serious. I need to go."

I push him aside, taking steps to walk away. He calls my name, unwillingly forcing me to stop. Taking a deep breath, I turn around and wait for him to revert to normal, tell me he drank too much, or apologize for his momentary lapse of judgment, but instead, he moves quickly to me and crashes his lips against mine with force. A moan escapes me, more of a desperate plea for him to back off as heat rises in my body. Pressing my hands back on his chest, I push him away, out of breath.

"To quote your partner, the one who got away, but now she's mine." He breathes so close to my mouth, I can almost taste him again. "You never could break away from me, Kate, so perhaps you've been mine all along."

He walks away with a satisfied smile, but not before leaving me standing alone with his careless thoughts. I hate the truth behind his words. Perhaps, throughout our forbidden affair, I always came back because I can't let go.

And in just one night, all my worlds have come crashing down again.

I'm back to three years ago, fighting my feelings for a man so unattainable and equally trying to maintain a friendship with someone else.

They say you're supposed to be wiser with age. I'll argue that in a heartbeat, I'm back in the same old mess.

The only way to solve the problem for tonight would be to enjoy the free liquor—the answer to everything.

But denial will only get me so far. I've protected myself for as long as I can and created this untouchable side to me, which no one can reach. And deep down inside, I know my time will run out.

Heartbreak is imminent.

TEN

KATE

We stumble out of the ballroom and back into the gardens.

Partygoers are loitering in the area, many like us—intoxicated and barely able to walk. Some people are loud, still in party mode, while others look completely wiped out. Several choose to unwind near the fire pit, sitting in groups as dawn sets in, the promise of a new day setting in the morning sky.

A large number of people drag their tired feet along the pebble-stone path, leaving the grounds after what has been one hell of a night.

The four of us sit with the others around the fire, watching its flames burn against the fresh morning air. After Dominic's interruption and Noah's outburst, the night should've gone downhill from there.

Until Lex bought the most expensive scotch and forced us to taste it. I tasted scotch several times, not minding it so much, though it was never my first choice to drink. Charlie, on the other hand, absolutely despises it.

Nevertheless, scotch and champagne don't mix. We're beyond walking straight, which doesn't matter since our time was spent on the dance floor. We laughed until our lungs hurt while tears streamed from our eyes. Our carefree nature attracted strangers to join our circle and dance with us. We became best friends, promised never to lose touch, and sung so loud our throats burned from the constant strain.

Yet it all had to come to an end, and as we sit here trying to come down from the high, my feet throb in pain. I can barely swallow, a constant parched feeling inside my mouth that I'm unable to shake even as I drink water to rehydrate.

The space around me has finally stopped spinning, with reality becoming more and more apparent.

Dominic wants to leave his wife for me.

And Noah is back in my life.

How did this happen?

"How do we move our feet to the hotel?" Charlie whines, resting her head on Lex's shoulder, closing her eyes. "I'm so sore."

"Ten-minute walk," Lex reassures her, though looking weathered himself. "Our clothes and toiletries have been delivered. We can get in a few hours of sleep before the car arrives at midday."

We make the dreaded ten-minute walk toward the hotel. To make it less painful, we reminisce about the night, making fun of ourselves on the dance floor. The champagne and other drinks we consumed still run through our veins, making the walk difficult yet amusing at the same time. Noah trips over nothing. Charlie stops to puke into the fancy bushes aligning the path. When the hotel is finally in sight, we all sigh with relief and part ways to our rooms to catch a few hours of sleep.

The ride to Mr. Auvray's winery was the complete opposite.

It's a two-hour drive, but being utterly hungover on less than four hours' sleep warrants complete silence. Thankfully, I organized a driver predicting the three of us would be in this state before I even knew about Noah.

Noah is dead quiet. Wearing his sunglasses, his gaze lingers outside the window as does Charlie's. Lex is fiddling with his phone, but even he looks tired.

"Mr. Auvray's vineyard cultures one of France's best champagnes," I mention, lightening the mood. "The vineyard has been passed down through the generations. His great-grandparents were the original owners."

"I can't think of anything worse than champagne-tasting right now," Charlie groans, sliding in her seat.

"There's also cheese," I offer.

"I thought you hated cheese?"

"No, I love cheese. It doesn't mean I need to date someone who makes love to cheese. You're certainly grumpy when you're hungover."

Another groan escapes her before she pulls out her phone and types a text. Seconds later, my phone vibrates. I give it a few moments, not wanting Lex and Noah to get suspicious.

Charlie: *Lex insisted on drunk sex. I hate him right now. I want to die. I'm so tired.*

I hold back my laughter, not surprised one bit by her admission. With Noah quiet beside me, I send him a text to see how he's holding up, unsure if he still uses this number.

Me: *Are you still alive?*

He lifts his phone to read the text, typing fast before the text appears on my screen.

Noah: *Yes... just thinking quietly, so shut up.*

Some things between us never change. I decide not to push him further, sliding my phone into my purse and diverting my attention back onto the scenery.

"What's wrong?" Charlie questions, annoyed at our secret exchange. "What did Noah say?"

"I, um..." I turn to Noah to answer as we're caught in the act. "I don't know what you're talking about."

"What's the secret between you? We're all friends, so spill."

"If we're all friends," Lex repeats with his head still focused on his screen. "Why don't you share what you sent Kate?"

"Fine," she huffs with exaggeration. "I'm exhausted, no thanks to you. Drunk sex is overrated, whereas sleep is not."

"If you think drunk sex is overrated, explain the two orgasms you had within minutes?"

Charlie's mouth falls to open the same time Noah groans, resting his head against the glass window.

"Driver, how long until we're there?" Noah almost shouts.

The driver smiles as we turn down another long road. "One hour, monsieur."

And that's the end of us talking during the car ride.

An hour later, Auvray Le Champagne is in view. There's something to be said about the countryside, it brings with it a sense of peace and serenity. Something I didn't realize was missing from my life of late until now.

Mr. Auvray is standing out front with his wife, Claudette, waving to us as the car pulls into the large circular driveway. With welcoming smiles, we all shake hands as I introduce everyone to him and his wife. Moments later, he motions for his staff to take our bags and offers to take us in for an introduction drink. The plan is to take a personal tour of the grounds later this afternoon, followed by a specially cooked dinner by his personal chef.

We choose to spend the few hours we have to spare exploring the town of Champagne. There's so much to see catering to different tastes—several bars from intimate and cozy to more sophisticated establishments that draw in a diverse crowd.

The finest wines and champagne are the region's specialties, along with the fantastic food each venue has to offer—a la carte menus and local culinary delicacies, a foodie's dream with all the choices to suit any pallet.

Yet, looking beyond the bars and restaurants, Champagne arouses the senses and showcases the best of France. It's easy for our eyes to feast on vines parading up the hillsides, the smell of fresh air so easy to breathe in. Everything is beautiful, and as we walk along the streets admiring our surroundings, Noah clears his throat beside me.

"Listen, about last night..."

I smile at a couple walking toward us, shuffling closer to Noah to avoid running into them. "What's going on with you?"

Noah bows his head, keeping his hands tucked in the pockets of his jeans. He often raises his eyes to gaze ahead but will quickly revert to his closed state.

"I don't know," he finally admits as Lex and Charlie turn around, suggesting we stop at the small café to grab some coffee.

The intense dark coffee is exactly what my body needs to sober up before we go champagne tasting later on today. Savoring those first few sips, my lips relish in delight as the warm liquid graces them.

After another hour of walking, my feet are on the verge of being numb. The caffeine begins to wear off as we make our way back to the chateau, making me incredibly grumpy. Sleep would be the perfect solution if Mr. Auvray weren't standing out front waiting for us to commence our tour.

The property is stunning. The architecture is exquisite, hand-built by his great-grandfather and uncle almost a century ago. Over the years, Mr. Auvray has spent some money updating the property, but it still can use some improvements to attract more guests.

We walk through the fields while Mr. Auvray explains the harvesting of the grapes to fermentation. He takes us through the production facility, showing us the remaining process all the way to corking. Finally, he then walks us through the dark cellars where bottles of champagne lay flat on their side labeled as vintage.

Lex is consumed with the entire process, asking questions as they walk slightly ahead of us. Noah walks beside me, kicking loose stones with his feet. I assume, much like me, the exhaustion has crept in explaining the uninviting mood.

"You've changed," Noah mutters, his words barely audible. "You're not the same person."

"Well, neither are you," I shoot back, annoyed at his judgmental tone. "Just because we were friends years ago doesn't mean it can go back to being the same."

"Wow, cold much?"

I stop dead in my tracks. "What's that supposed to mean?"

"You've turned into this career-driven woman, no time for men or anyone. Actually, I stand corrected. You clearly have time to fuck Dominic, am I correct?"

Crossing my arms against my chest, the thrum of my pulse is fast and rapid, my stomach hardening from the truth coming out. My stare remains fixed, eyes never leaving Noah's judgmental stance. "I don't know what you're talking about."

"Of course not, your life. I get it."

"How dare you judge me?" My voice smolders with resentment. "I'm certain your marriage breakdown has something to do with you being an arrogant prick!"

The words echo in the cellar, but thankfully Mr. Auvray, Lex, and Charlie have stepped out.

Noah shakes his head, narrowing his eyes while curling his lip. "You're just like her."

"Excuse me?"

"Driven by ambition, and you'll do anything to keep it that way."

I point my finger at him, unsure how he managed to evoke so much emotion from me. "Firstly, don't compare me to your wife. What I choose to do with my personal life is none of your business. In fact, I never asked you to come here. It was Charlie's idea, not mine. I was happy without you in my life."

With the drop of his head and hands in his pocket, Noah turns his back and walks away. My words were callous, a clear heat-of-the-moment exchange, and the further he walks away, regret finds its way to me like a gust of wind after the remnants of a storm.

Lex and Charlie are waiting at the entrance, noticing Noah missing. I quickly let them know I'm heading to my room for a rest before joining them for dinner. Back in my room, I throw myself onto my bed, willing my eyes to close. But sleep is impossible, and Noah's words haunt me to no avail. So, I changed, big deal. And who cares if I'm ambitious, I've been this way since before I met him. His opinion is his opinion. I just have no idea why it matters so much to me.

Why do I even care?

My eyes close, but the weight on my mind only allows me to shut down for a few minutes. I've grown accustomed to power naps while I travel, a quick way to re-energize. I decide to take a long shower to ease my tense muscles, but no matter how hard I try, my mind shuffles back and forth between Noah and Dominic. Two very different men in my life wanting different things.

I hop out, frustrated at myself for overthinking and dress into a sleek slate-colored cocktail dress which sits mid-thigh, flaring at the waist with an off-the-shoulder design. Pairing the dress with black strappy Alexander McQueen heels, the necklace I wear is simple with matching hooped earrings and an oval turquoise ring to add a splash of color. Finishing off my face, my makeup is simple, and my hair is tied back into a tight ponytail.

Staring into the mirror, I take a deep breath until my phone buzzes in front of me.

Dominic's name appears with a video file attached. My fingers move faster than my brain rationalizing and telling me don't open it.

The video begins with Dominic lying on the bed completely naked with his cock standing upright, rock hard. He begins to stroke it, slowly, his face wincing as if every stroke brings him pleasure and pain. The hairs on my arms begin to rise, the temperature in the room increases to an uncomfortable level of heat. Shaking my head, willing to break me from his hold, I hit pause on the video and throw my phone on the bed in frustration.

Dinner is to be served outside on the large terrace with open views of the vineyard. The sun is yet to set as I step out, but still, the scenery takes my breath away.

Lex and Charlie are already sitting down along with Mr. Auvray and Claudette. Taking a seat on the opposite side of Charlie, she offers a smile before Noah joins us.

My eyes fall upon him, the way he looks so handsome in a pair of black trousers and a navy-blue dress shirt. The dinner isn't overly formal, prompting him to roll up his sleeves with his shirt slightly unbuttoned, exposing his chest. The smell of his cologne lingers in the air, creating this unwanted feeling inside of me. Perhaps I've been too harsh on him, adding stress to his life when it's evident he's going through something significant.

Beneath the table, I move my hand toward his and place it on top, squeezing it tight to let him know it'll be okay. He doesn't flinch nor turn my way, but beneath my hand, his muscles relax.

Mr. Auvray spends most of the dinner educating us on the history of the winery.

The food is delicious—French delicacies and, of course, more cheese. The three of us verbally agree for Lexed to invest in the business, seeing its potential and the passion the Auvray's have toward maintaining its integrity.

"I'll organize a meeting this week and gather my team to

begin working on this project," I inform Mr. Auvray. "I'd also like my management team, who will be working closely with you, to come visit so they can experience all of this for themselves."

Raising his glass, he welcomes us to join him. "*Un toast à notre avenir!*"

We toast to our future, our glasses clinking against each other until it's Noah's against mine. With a warm smile, Noah's face softens as we drink more champagne.

After several courses are served, we retreat to the outside area with our glasses. There's a beautiful stone fire pit that sits in the middle of an open space, surrounded by soft lounge chairs. It's a beautiful night out of the city, stars twinkling with a summer breeze cooling our skin.

"I've fallen in love with this place," Charlie murmurs, nestling her head against Lex's chest. "France is beautiful."

"Perhaps we can purchase a chateau and bring the girls here for the summer?" Lex suggests.

Charlie sits up with a grin. "How very Angelina Jolie of you. But are you serious?"

"Why not? Money's not an object. With Kate here, she can use the place whenever she feels like, and Mom loves France. Even Adriana could come to stay if she'd like."

"Oh my gosh, okay, there's so much to think about." Charlie's excitement picks up, prompting her to place her glass down.

"Okay, calm down." Lex smiles, stretching his arms with a yawn escaping. "I need sleep while you scour Pinterest like usual."

The two of them call it a night, leaving Noah and me by ourselves as they walk back, holding hands with Charlie giggling. Seeing them together still brings me joy. After what they went through years ago, it's clear that they were always destined to be together despite what life threw at them. I'm not a strong believer in the whole 'soulmate' thing, but I swear they're soulmates. They complement each other yet never sacrifice their beliefs for the sake of staying together. They follow their passions, and at the end of the day, share their lives while raising a beautiful family. I've always admired the way Charlie makes it all work and respects Lex for his commitment toward his family.

In the air, the sound of nature is somewhat comforting, but sooner or later, we will have to talk.

"Noah, I'm sorry about earlier today. I had no right to blame you for your marriage. It was rude and uncalled for."

He releases a sigh, taking a drink. "Me, too. I could blame the shots last night or lack of sleep, but it's all an excuse."

I pour him more champagne and some for myself. Resting my back against the chair, my gaze lingers toward the night sky, the blank canvas a refreshing break from the chaos we've both been trying to fight against.

"What happened to you and Morgan?" I whisper, keeping my stare fixed on the sky, hoping I'm not smothering him with my curiosity.

"We fell apart," he draws out in a long breath. "She wanted our marriage to work one way, and I wanted it another way. We tried to compromise, but all we did was fight."

"And now?"

"She handed me divorce papers, Kate. And the same night she did that, I was beyond hurt and made a mistake."

"A mistake?"

"I slept with someone."

"Oh."

"Well, I sort of knew her but not really. To get to the point, she fell pregnant. I have a son, Nash."

I almost choke on my wine, making a gurgling sound as Noah pats my back hard. Sitting up, I turn to face him. "Let me get this straight. Morgan hands you divorce papers, so you screw what's her—"

"Olivia," he interrupts.

"Olivia, and she gave birth to your son? But how?"

"Ask the universe. The condom must have broken. I was angry at Morgan. I don't know, Kate. It's done, okay?"

By just the sound of his voice, I can hear the pain from his open wound, the blood so effortlessly pouring out with every breath he takes. There's so much to take in, and now, Charlie makes sense. Noah Mason is a broken man, tormenting himself over a mistake with dire consequences. Questions are flooding my thoughts, each one fighting for attention. But I try to control myself, asking only what's necessary rather than get into the semantics of it all.

"How did Morgan take it? The news about Olivia?"

"How do you think?"

"Noah, I don't understand how you and Morgan fell apart. You have a daughter, Jessa, right?"

He nods, clasping his hands. I can see his struggle, the way his emotions sting causing a pained stare into the dark night.

"She wants her career over staying with Jessa. Both our jobs are demanding, and the more we began squabbling over the small things, the bigger they became. I can't change who she is. Her sister, Scarlett, will always be her number one priority. I just thought when we had Jessa, things would change," his voice croaks, the vulnerability in his admission leaving a heavy feeling all over me. "Between her stepson, Michael, Jessa, and Scarlett, there isn't time left for me.

Morgan has always been the carer for many people, and I respect that, but I want a wife who will be by my side when I propose marriage. I don't expect to have to vie for her attention."

I nod my head, listening to him pour his heart out. With so many people involved, it's never going to be easy, but quite possibly Noah's biggest mistake is thinking he can change who Morgan is.

"And who initiated the separation?" I ask.

"Her. I thought it would be good given how toxic we had become, and time apart would help us see what we want, but it has driven us further apart. The papers blind-sided me on Christmas Eve, out of all nights."

"I'm sorry," is all I can say.

"After that night, Morgan reached out to me to try to make it work, and I wanted to try for the sake of Jessa. We were together for four months. We attended marriage counseling, then Olivia texted me. I fucked up, Kate." Noah buries his head into his hands, trying to hide the anguish.

"Hey." I reach my hand out and touch his arm. "You didn't fuck up. This is life. We make good decisions, and we make bad ones."

He raises his head with bloodshot eyes, the vacant stare behind the normally bright hazel orbs worries me to no avail.

"I'm too old to be making bad decisions. I have two kids."

"You're never too old to make bad decisions," I tell him. "But sometimes those bad decisions end up being the path to something right. I'm not going to pretend to understand, but you'll get through this. You're strong, Noah."

"I hope you're right."

I lay back down on the chair. "I'm always right."

Noah shakes his head, a smile finally escaping his lips. "Typical French, so arrogant."

"I'll take that as a compliment." Letting out a yawn, I decide to call it a night, noting it's late. "I need to sleep. Will you be okay out here?"

"*Mieux vaut être seul que mal accompagné*," he says with a smile.

"Better to be alone than in bad company?" I translate with a playful grin. "Since when do you speak French? Plus, I resent that. I'm only bad in the States, specifically Malibu, on the beach. In France, I'm an angel."

Noah's eyes dance with delight, the familiar flicker returning as his lips simper. "Sure. Good night, Kate."

I stand—slightly dizzy from the champagne—to head back to my room but stop in my tracks. "Noah, you were right. About the whole Dominic thing. I'm not perfect, just like you. We all make mistakes, no matter how adult we think we are at times."

I expect Noah to give me a lecture on self-worth, or better yet, a list of reasons why I shouldn't be fucking a married guy who owns a sex club, but it never comes. Instead, he continues to lay, staring at the stars.

"Of course, I'm right. I still know you better than anyone else."

His words resonate and hold so much truth. I never realized how much I miss conversing with an adult, and especially how much I miss Noah. And before heading to bed, I raise my eyes to meet with the stars.

Somewhere in this crazy universe of ours, someone is playing a game. The dice have been rolled, and the next move could determine everything or maybe nothing at all.

Dominic wants more, and Noah needs—I'm not sure. The uncertainty of him walking back into my life complicates everything. This time though, I vow not to let my emotions think we're anything but long-lost friends.

Strictly platonic—the way it was always meant to be with Noah and me.

As for Dominic, I'll soon have to face the music of exactly where that will head.

ELEVEN

KATE

S leep can do wondrous things when you manage to get some.

All four of us are in much better spirits the next morning, enjoying our breakfast before our trip back to Paris. The Auvray's head chef, Archille, spoiled us with homemade pastries and a spread of delicious breakfast foods, all of which tasted amazing. Even Lex is impressed, questioning Archille on where he saw himself in the future. I can almost see the wheels turning in Lex's head. He has an eye for talent and knows exactly when to strike.

The plan is to take Monday off to spend time with Charlie while Lex attends some meetings. I should've known better. No matter how hard I try to prepare to take some time off, work always finds me. My phone pings like crazy, email after email, and calls from people who panicked while I was absent.

My assistant, Emile, reassures me everything is being handled. She reminds me of my young self, which is why I hired her when I moved to Paris. Upon offering her the position, a generous salary came with it in hopes of keeping her for the long haul. Even Lex is impressed by how efficient she is. When Lex offers such a compliment, you take it with pride.

I've rather been enjoying the company, but with my eyes glued to the screen, the urgent emails need attention. My thumbs type quickly to answer what I can until a text pops up on the top of my screen.

Dominic: *Tonight, please. Our usual. We need to talk.*

My eyes read over his words as if they will change by the sheer power of my thoughts. I opt not to respond, lifting my head with a forced smile and ignoring the pressure from his request. Noah is watching me with a curious gaze behind his coffee cup, his beard somewhat of a novelty to me. With the rest we all deserved, he appears more like the man I remember him to be—handsome and sexy with an arrogance only he can get away with. And behind all that is the best friend who would make me laugh, stroke my hair, and tell me everything would be just fine. He argued with me over the most trivial things, but that's what bonded us in the end.

"You're looking at me oddly," he claims, grabbing another pastry. "If you're going to argue the beard, I'll have you know it's a lady magnet."

"A lady magnet?" I purse my lips to hold back my smile. "Because you need more ladies in your life?"

"Hmm... you have a strong point."

"You're still as dashing as ever, Noah Mason," I tell him with a twinkle in my eye while reacting to his sardonic grin. "And arrogant, painful... the list can go on."

"It's okay. I think you've made yourself perfectly clear.

You think I'm an arrogantly handsome man who you want to have sex with, right?"

I throw a piece of pastry at him. "You're impossibly annoying."

"Listen here." Charlie breaks us up, wiping her mouth with the fancy napkin. "Before the two of you consummate on this table, can we talk about the rest of today? Kate and I are shopping in Paris this afternoon. What are your plans, Noah?"

"He's busy with me," Lex interjects, his expression blank and unreadable. "We have something we need to look at."

"Chatte Française..." Charlie mumbles beneath her breath.

Lex presses his lips together and puts down his coffee to turn to Charlie. "No, it's not French pussy. There are a few people I'd like Noah to meet as well. A potential opportunity for us back in the States."

I bow my head to hold back my comments. Lex sure has the patience for Charlie, though I wouldn't put it past them to stumble into a Parisian strip joint, especially since Noah is now single.

On our ride back to Paris, we talk about business, the beautiful scenery, to Eric's nagging messages about all the gossip from the ball. Charlie briefly mentions seeing Dominic, and Eric proceeds to complain and call him a moron for not attending his parents' anniversary dinner. Translated, Eric is jealous that he didn't think to try to get out of it and complains it was a bunch of his parents' old friends.

As the city's familiar sights come to full view, Charlie talks about shopping again as Lex rolls his eyes in boredom. He casually mentions that work may take a bit longer than expected. Surprisingly, Charlie negotiates her shopping time in line with his work time, then a late stroll around Paris, followed by dinner. I was torn somewhere in the middle, wanting to join Lex in the office and spend time with Charlie. Until Noah brought up spending the night together which I agreed to since it's his last night in town.

I decide to head into the office with Lex for two hours before joining Charlie for a late lunch and shopping, then dinner with Noah. That way, everyone will be happy.

The two hours fly by quickly, and as usual, the staff panics in Lex's presence. I have no idea why, he's much nicer to people than BC—Before Charlie.

With that behind me, I race to meet Charlie at the Boulevard Haussmann and the Grands Boulevards, known for housing old Parisian department stores and selling top designer collections for men and women, gourmet food shopping, home design, jewelry, and so many other things.

Charlie is in heaven, dragging me to each store and boutique, where she enjoys browsing and picking up a few pieces. When we enter La Perla, I'm no stranger to the sexy lingerie on display, having purchased a few items from here.

"Would you look at this?" Charlie picks up a strappy piece of string supposed to be a one piece of some sort. "You could really floss your bits with a piece like this."

We both laugh in unison. I pick up a bustier, admiring the intricate lace and beading.

"So, we didn't get a chance to discuss Dominic and his wife." Charlie watches me with curiosity.

I purposely distract myself by sorting through the rack, looking for my size. "What's there to discuss? I was just as surprised to see him there as you were."

"You're telling me you still don't talk to him?" Her tone is unforgiving, and her perfectly straight posture standing beside me is supposed to intimidate me. I know her tactics well. "You know, you're a terrible liar."

"Charlie," I say, willing to come up with a lie, but the guilt begins to wreck me. "It's not what you think."

Charlie's eyes widen with concern. "Not what I think? I think the two of you have something on the side. I think Dominic seeing you with Noah sparked some jealousy in him. I also think... sorry, I also know, Noah can't stand the guy."

How on earth does she come up with all that? Remember, she's a lawyer and excellent at reading people. There's a psychology to being so intuitive and making a career from it.

"I don't want to discuss this."

"Of course, you don't. Dominic is probably in panic mode, trying to get you to continue being his mistress. And you're scared."

"I'm not scared, okay?" I sputter in defense. "We agreed to one simple rule, and he wants to break it. Charlie, I'm not like you. I don't want the whole family and babies. I'm happy with my life the way it is. Yes, I enjoy sex with no attachments, and sure, it would be nice to have a companion. But I'm not interested in complicated relationships. If a man wants to be with me, and I want to be with him without all the drama, then great."

"It's not always that easy." Charlie disagrees while shaking her head. "Sometimes, with love, you've got to go through the heartbreak to have your happily ever after."

"I have gone through heartbreak," I remind her. "Multiple times. And I'd rather not set myself up for that again."

"When the right guy comes along, it may be unavoidable. It'll consume you like a spell, no matter how hard you try to escape. There's no way out. Kismet. Soulmates."

"You're such a hopeless romantic." I laugh, eyeing the

outfit in her hand. "Yet at the same time, a kinky whore. Are you buying the flosser because I'm hungry and need something to eat?"

"Yeah, I'll buy the flosser. Lex will be in for a real treat tonight." Charlie chuckles softly then quiets down, placing her hand on my arm gently. "But seriously, Kate, I'm worried about you. You're all alone here. Paris is beautiful but wouldn't it be more amazing with someone who you could spend the rest of your life with?"

"Charlie, I'm happy with my life. Yeah, it's nice to have you guys around, but I'm always busy. It's not like I'm alone every day."

"It's nice to have Noah around?" She raises her brows, waiting for me to respond.

"It's been a while. Noah has a lot on his mind."

"So, he told you?"

"He told me everything."

"And?"

"And what?"

Charlie lets out a sigh. "What do you make of it all?"

I think long and hard about her question. While the news comes as a shock, the predicament he now finds himself in is more of a concern.

"I guess, if I'm honest, he needs to man-up and be responsible. He made a mistake, and now he needs to live with that decision."

"But don't you feel sorry for him? I mean, the poor guy can't catch a break. I have my feelings about Morgan, but who am I to give my opinion on his marriage? It just had cracks well before the 'I do.' I always thought that he and you..." Charlie trails off.

I stop and turn her way. "Him and me what? Should've been together?"

Charlie simply nods.

"You know my stance on that. We may have been best friends, but we're two completely different people. If we were meant to be, that would've happened four years ago. It didn't, so there's your answer."

"You're just like Lex in so many ways," Charlie openly complains. "It's not so black and white when it comes to relationships. I just think you and Noah have always had this special bond."

"And I think this matter should be closed," I tell her forcefully. "Noah has his hands full with his daughter and son. I'm sure, and much like me, he doesn't have time for anything else. Now, let's go to lunch because I'm starving."

Shopping with Charlie is utterly exhausting. Her excitement stems from being child-free and not wanting to waste a single moment. After our trip to La Perla, we make our way back to the hotel and find Noah in the lobby.

"Nice dent in the credit card?"

"We're in Paris, Noah. It's a given," Charlie informs him. "I'm going upstairs to change for dinner, but I'll see you for breakfast before we fly out?"

I nod, shifting my gaze back to Noah, who's staring at the La Perla bag.

"What's in the bag?"

"A croissant," I lie, jokingly.

"A croissant? I mean, look, I know you were excited to see me, but I had no clue you were dressing up."

"You're annoying, and I'm tired. Mind if we head to my place so I can change?"

"Into your croissant?"

"I think I remember why I stopped hanging out with you…"

Ten minutes later, we're inside my apartment. Noah is

busily scanning the living room, admiring the place with an impressive nod as he walks through.

"Some place you've got," Noah compliments before moving toward the balcony. "I can understand why you don't want to leave. It's incredibly beautiful here and some view, huh?"

"It is..." I say, removing my wedges.

I tell him I'll be back, hopping into the shower quickly, then changing into my white sundress. With my hair loose, just sitting past my shoulders, and changing my wedges for my strappy tanned heels, I grab another purse before entering the living room.

"Beautiful," he breathes as the corner of his lips turn up. "As always."

"You're sucking up to me. Did you break a vase while out here?"

"Let's go." He chuckles. "Show me Paris at night."

We walk the streets and watch the city evolve into nightlife. Stopping at a quaint restaurant, we talk about life and work. It's not hard to see that Noah loves his kids, showing me pictures of Jessa and talking about her milestones. Since Nash is only a few weeks old, he doesn't have as much to say about him.

"Being a father suits you," I profess to him, fondly. "I can tell you adore them."

"They're every reason to be alive," he claims, staring at his phone. "It's really hard, you know, being apart from Jessa and this co-parenting business. Morgan can be quite difficult. As for Nash, it still feels new. I don't feel like I've quite bonded with him just yet."

"Jessa looks exactly like you." I smile, noting the similarities. "Has your eyes."

"I think she looks like her mother."

"Noah." I rest my hand on his, trying to understand again how this all went pear-shaped on him, but my phone vibrates, and the name Dominic appears on my screen. I should open it, but the second that I do, I know that my focus will shift to a man who doesn't deserve my attention right now.

"You want to answer that?" Noah retracts his hand, motioning for my phone.

"No," I tell him firmly. "I'm here with you."

Noah looks less than amused, unable to make eye contact with me. I don't bother to ask him his problem when I know he can read between the lines.

We finish our dinner, then walk the streets to the Eiffel Tower. Tourists surround us, admiring the light show with endless pictures to save the memories of visiting Paris.

After not talking for almost ten minutes, Noah turns to face me. "I'm sorry, Kate. For how I ended things between us. I don't know why I felt I had to choose between you and Morgan."

"You were in love..." I murmur with my eyes fixed on the sight before us.

"Kate, it wasn't just that."

"Noah, please, let's just enjoy this rather than dwell on the past. It's done."

We watch the rest of the show until a cool breeze causes me to shiver. I probably should've brought something to wear on top of my dress, not expecting the temperature to drop so drastically. Noah places his arms around my waist and pulls me into his side as if no time has passed between us.

"I missed you, and us, and more importantly, just being me," he admits quietly. "I feel like I've lost so much of myself."

I should push him away because with his arms around me, my feelings begin to shift to this unwanted place. Yes, it's nice to have the comfort of a man, but that's it.

He's just a friend. Always remember that.

"This is nice," I whisper, leaning my head on his shoulder until my phone begins to vibrate again. I pull it out of my pocket and see the same name pop up on my screen at the same time Noah purposely looks.

"Why don't you answer him, Kate? Tell him it's over."

"Over?" I pull away, not liking Noah's tone. "Dominic and I are nothing, so there's nothing to be over."

"C'mon, it's me. If this friendship is to work, we need honesty."

"Do you still love Morgan?" I blurt out as his arm falls beneath me. "If she stood in front of you right now and wanted to reconcile, would you take her back?"

"It's not that simple," he grits. "We're beyond repair, okay? I made sure of that the night I fucked Olivia."

"You didn't answer my question. Do you still love Morgan?"

Noah doesn't answer my question, his mood shifting immediately. "And if Dominic wants an exclusive relationship with you, would you say yes?"

"That's the problem," I mumble. "And if you want honesty, then here goes, I never wanted that from him. I learned to take the good and leave the bad."

"So, you fuck him, and that's it?" Noah grunts.

He makes it sound worse than it is. Or maybe, just maybe, it does appear that way. Yes, he satisfies me sexually, but Noah repeating the facts to me makes it sound ten times worse.

"Look, okay, we both got a lot going on. It's great you

came, but I'm not the same Kate you became friends with years ago."

"You're right," Noah says, pulling away. "The Kate I loved would never have degraded herself to a man who offers her nothing but shame."

Noah begins to walk away, leaving me to stand alone with his harsh words.

And a call from Dominic waiting to be answered.

TWELVE

KATE

An empty feeling in the pit of my stomach grows larger with every step closer toward the hotel.

As I stand outside the main doors, I stop and stare at the building before me, giving myself a few moments to regroup. Behind the doors is a man who will use his power to control the energy around us in his favor. Yet for years, we've been sneaking around, allowing him to do just that, and it never bothered me. Until now.

My lips press together in a slight grimace, struggling to take the next step forward. On top of my already heightened nerves, my earlier argument with Noah only adds to the stress of it all. I hate the fact that I'm even thinking about him right now. All of a sudden, he strolls back into my life, and I'm supposed to factor in his opinion?

You hate that he's right.

With my shoulders back while inhaling a deep breath, my feet move forward and through the doors into the lobby. I agreed to meet him at the bar inside the hotel rather than the room. It was that or nothing. Despite his resistance to doing so, he finally agreed.

The bar is located just near the main desk, small with dim lighting creating an intimate environment for patrons enjoying a drink. The walls are a deep red with velvet chairs in the same color scattered around the round tables inside. Toward the back corner is a booth where Dominic is sitting. His head is bowed, and the thick black mane of hair which is normally styled perfectly, looks messy and misplaced. The weight of his gaze is fixated on the tumbler in his hands. As I move closer, the amber liquid appears to be whisky—his choice of drink.

I slide into the booth, his head rising to meet my eyes, though without a greeting or even a welcoming smile. Sitting on the table is a glass of wine he pre-ordered. Raising the glass toward my lips, I drink the entire contents before even speaking.

"I never explained to you why I married Allegra."

"You said you got scared," I so easily remind him.

"Yes, I did, to an extent," he admits with a hoarse voice. "About five years ago, I helped an old friend of mine who was in trouble financially. I was naïve to think loaning the money would've solved the problem. He owed the wrong people, and when they found out I had some tie to him, I was on their radar."

I'd heard the story too often in the corporate world— corrupt dealings, hands in the black market, all sorts of trouble which is fatal to any reputable business.

Dominic runs his finger along the edge of the glass before continuing, "Allegra's father offered me a lifeline... marry his daughter, and the problem will disappear."

"So, your marriage is somewhat a business deal. Is that what you're trying to tell me?"

He simply nods his head, keeping his words at bay. "Kate, I want you, but ending my marriage is complicated."

"But where's this coming from? I don't understand, Dominic. You made it clear from the beginning that you didn't do relationships. Period."

"You don't understand love?"

I never in my wildest dreams expected Dominic to say the four-letter word. When told in the right circumstances, this word can seal your future, fill it with joy and happiness. And then there are moments like now when a man carelessly uses the word like it means nothing.

Staring at the table, I have nothing positive to say right now. A sudden feeling of heaviness expands within me, causing my muscles to turn numb. I'm unable to smile, laugh, cry, or evoke any emotion besides shock.

Dominic places his hand on mine, a loving gesture, unlike his usually distant self. "I think about you all day and all night. When she's lying beside me in bed, I picture it being you. It always comes back to you. I've never felt this way before. It's driving me fucking crazy."

The desperation in his tone is difficult to ignore, along with the heavy weight of his hand on mine.

"And then I see you with him? It kills me to see you with someone else. That's when I realized I can't do this anymore. I don't want another man touching you. I want you to be all mine."

I drag my hand back toward my lap, the hurt on his face evident.

"So, this is about Noah? Are you jealous? Let me guess. Your ego has taken a hit, so now you think that telling me you feel something is going to make me do what, exactly?"

"Not something, I love you, Kate," he finally admits.

My skin begins to flush, and the room becomes incredibly hot all of a sudden. With my lips pulled back baring my teeth, I stand quickly, willing this conversation to end. "I need to go. This conversation is over. Sort out your marriage, Dominic, but don't make decisions based on what you think you feel."

I storm out of the bar, not turning around to watch him try to intimidate me, and through the lobby back onto the street. The threat of rain lingers in the air. I keep my head down, trying to shut out the noise on the solemn walk home. After several blocks, the pitter-patter of the rain begins to create a shield around me. The drops fall hard, soaking my hair and clothes while cooling my skin. The beads trickle down my face, washing away the uncertainty of my life, if only for a few moments.

In the space of a week, my simple life went from zero to a hundred.

Noah's back.

Dominic professes the word love.

And all of this complicates my life no matter which way I turn.

I'm damned if I do, and damned if I don't.

My pace slows against the unpredictable storm which lashes our city. The strands of my hair cling onto my skin, a sticky and uncomfortable feeling which is rampant with the humidity. In the reflection of the glass, my makeup is strewn. The so-called waterproof mascara has left me with panda eyes. Fumbling inside my bag for my keys, I lift my head and see Noah standing against the wall beside my door.

"What are you doing here?" I ask, catching my breath.

"Waiting for you. I wanted to apologize for what I said tonight, but perhaps I'm the idiot," his tone turns deep with resentment. "You went to him, didn't you?"

"See, this is why we can't be friends, Noah. What I do with my life is my choice. Not you or Charlie have any say. Just like I never once stopped you from marrying Morgan."

"I'm not stopping you from doing anything, okay? I'm pointing out that he's no good for you. You deserve better."

"I deserve to make my own choices. Now, if you'll excuse me, I'm drenched, drained and want to go to bed."

Finally, finding my keys, I jiggle them in the lock and open the door. Noah hovers at the entrance, and with my shoulders slumped, I pull him in without saying a word.

In a sudden move, he wraps his arms around me in a tight embrace. As my face falls onto his chest, inhaling his scent, I beg myself not to cry in his presence. I can't even recall the last time I shed a tear. I'm not an emotionally driven person, and tonight has fucked with my entire belief system.

"Remember when you told me we all make mistakes?" he whispers softly. "Just a mistake, Kate. Move on."

In the time we were apart, I forgot what it was like to have someone who knows the pits of my soul, who understands my resistance to fail and knows precisely how to make me move forward to better things.

Noah has always done this until, of course, I was pushed aside.

My hands fall flat against his chest, creating distance as I avoid his stare.

"Go shower. Then we're watching a movie and ordering takeout," he demands with a warm smile. "I need some American food because I'm missing it like crazy."

I drop my head with a soft chuckle. "So that you know, we're watching *The Breakfast Club* tonight."

"Is it about breakfast and eating?"

"No, consider it a rite of passage into adulthood."

"I think I've heard that before." He smirks.

"And before you ask, yes, it's the same actress as in *Pretty in Pink*."

I step away to the sound of his groan. Taking a quick shower to wash tonight off me, I throw on a pair of gray bed shorts and a matching tank. I brush my hair aside, letting it dry naturally as I head back to the living room.

Noah's eyes turn as I sit down beside him.

"What?" I ask, grabbing the remote.

"You're half-naked on me."

"I'm not half-naked on you. This is bedwear from a very expensive boutique in Italy."

"I can literally see all of your tits."

My hands cover my chest while I turn to face him in shock.

"You're such a man. The fabric isn't see-through." I remove my hands, trying to prove a point. "See?"

Noah's face strains. "What do they charge you for a piece of fabric which barely covers you, and also, are you cold?"

I grab the pillow, smacking him with it, which causes my strap to slide and an accidental nip slip. "Oh, sod off!"

Noah laughs. "The Brit is back. And just so you know, ready when you are but with those girls on show, I probably won't last long."

"Hey, ground rules, buddy," I remind him. "We're just friends. The sexual innuendo stops here."

"Can I make one more comment about your nipples?"

"No." I yawn while using the remote. "I get it. I have big tits. Now shut up."

"Is your yawn an indication of how boring the movie will be?"

I smack his arm. "Just watch, no questions."

Only ten minutes into the film, he clears his throat.

"Can I ask just one question?" he begs with his eyes and a naughty smile.

I pause the film, turning to face him with an annoyed glare.

"How much did you miss me?" He grins.

Unable to hide my smile, I nudge him before resting my head on his shoulder.

"No more questions," I tell him before whispering. "And a lot. More than you can ever imagine."

THIRTEEN

KATE

"I'm really going to miss this place."

Charlie slaps a decent serving of French jam onto her pastry, moaning as she takes a bite. If I didn't know better, she's eating for two, though the copious amounts of alcohol consumed over the weekend would eliminate that idea.

"The place or the food?" I question her while drinking coffee, enjoying the warm liquid to pass through my mouth and ignite all my senses. "Are you sure you're not pregnant?"

Charlie stops mid-bite, turning toward me with her mouth wide open. "Don't you dare jinx me. Three girls are enough. Some women are built for large families, I'm barely able to use the toilet without being interrupted."

Lex nods his head with a knowing smirk. "I'm going to agree with Charlotte on this, three is enough."

Noah appears uncomfortable, and I'm gathering the subject of children being a sore spot for him. We've only talked briefly about it over the weekend since every time the topic was raised, he asked to discuss something else. Last night, we spent hours talking about absolute nonsense until he left just after midnight. I didn't expect the idle chit-chat to be entertaining, but I haven't laughed so hard in a while without an alcoholic drink in hand.

"Sorry, Noah," Charlie murmurs, placing her food down. "Do you want to talk?"

"What's there to say?"

My gaze shifts between the two of them. Gathering by his withdrawn mood, I sense something has happened in the last few hours. I hold back on asking. If Noah wants to share, then he'll share, and I don't want to be the one to push him, especially in front of the present company.

We eat in silence until it becomes time for the three of them to leave. Outside on the street with their suitcases inside the car, I say goodbye to Lex but not before running over a few work matters. Charlie is standing beside him, dabbing the corner of her eye with a tissue.

"Come here, you big softy." I pull her into an embrace as she clutches onto me tightly.

"I know it's beautiful here," she whispers against my shoulder. "But it's not the same without you. We all miss you so much. Think about coming home, one day, please, when it's right."

And that's the thing about being home, I've always pictured it as a place where hopes and dreams come alive. Charlie's definition of home is where the heart lies, where the laughter carries, where friends belong, and where memories are made.

"But if I'm not here, you won't be able to set me up on awful blind dates with arrogant French men," I tease, lighting the mood.

Charlie's lips break out into a smile, a small laugh

escaping her. "I promise to do better. Well, actually, this time I did good, didn't I?"

She eyes Noah beside her, my head nodding in agreement. "I'll visit soon, promise."

"I'm going to hold you to that. Amelia's birthday is coming up, and it's not an alien party without you."

I cringe, jokingly. "Okay, I'm sure the boss will grant me some vacation time."

Charlie kisses my cheek before climbing into the car with Lex.

Noah is leaning with his back against the car, arms crossed, but his earlier worry disappears as his eyes light up while gazing at me. "You want to hug it out or something?"

I already miss him, trying to ignore the slight pang inside my heart from his departure. "You're a dork."

Stepping closer, he wraps his arms around me. Inside his embrace, my body warms at his touch, a familiar contentment I've missed in his absence. The mixed emotions of him leaving is swirling around in the pit of my stomach. It's silly to think I wish he could stay and selfish of me to beg him. Releasing me, he kisses my forehead the way he's done many times before.

"Noah, it'll work out," I say softly, doing my best to destroy the fear consuming him. "No matter what, you'll do the right thing."

"What if I don't?"

I pull away but still hold onto him. Behind the eyes of this beautiful man lays a battle only he can conquer. This weekend reminds me of the bond we once shared. We've both made mistakes in the past, and who am I to hold a grudge? I'm far from perfect.

"You've got me to set you straight," I remind him while staring into his eyes with a soft smile. "Now, go on that plane and spend time with your kids. I'll expect a photo of Jessa in the beret you bought. And don't forget to tell her Aunty Kate is so much more fun than Uncle Eric."

Noah shakes his head while laughing, touching my hand softly. This feeling is so strange yet alarmingly familiar at the same time. A simple gesture—a touch of the hand— stretches throughout my entire body, but rather than bring with it a sense of panic, it works the opposite and makes me *feel complete*.

And, in this moment, where I lose myself in my thoughts trying to decipher what this all means, he withdraws his hand, and I'm at an instant loss. Noah enters the car with a final wave until the black Mercedes drives off down the street, disappearing from my sight.

For years, I've mastered being alone, focusing on myself and making life into lemonade from the lemons I was handed. But saying goodbye to the three of them is harder than I ever thought it would be. I'm not sure exactly why as I've seen Lex numerous times over the years, though Charlie not as often unless we meet abroad. The two of them have become my family and welcomed me with open arms and always support my decisions. Their children feel like my own, their home is always open to me, and not once have I felt otherwise. Yet throwing Noah into the mix changes the dynamic. Charlie and Noah are family, by blood. They have a history and childhood none of us can match. When Noah came to LA, his bond with Lex tightened to brotherhood. I've known Lex long enough to know he respects and admires Noah's tenacity, believing he has what it takes to challenge himself with something bigger. Lex has become this family man, changing his values along the way.

And together, with the love which conquers all of us, our bonds have been tightened in more ways than one.

Over the next few days, I throw myself into work, trying to get back into a routine. Noah texts me daily, random trivia just like back in the day. Because of our time zones, we don't chat at night like we used to, but his texts make up for the nightly chat. It's fair to say I miss him despite his inappropriate advances and constant bringing up my breasts in conversation.

By Friday afternoon, I'm ready to call it a week. It must have been a full moon or something like it to warrant such idiotic behavior from my staff. Even clients are more demanding, less patient, and everyone seems on edge, especially me. It's almost like a storm is brewing on the horizon ready to hit landfall soon.

Taking a few days off caused more headaches than I realized. Just as I'm about to leave the office, Emile calls through, informing me of a visitor. I step outside my office to meet the eyes of Allegra.

Her style is sophisticated—an ivory pencil dress with a thick black belt above her waist. The pumps she wears are Louboutin, of course, and in her hand, she clutches tightly her prize possession—her Birkin bag.

"Kate, can we speak somewhere private?"

"Of course."

With every step back into my office, my heart rate spikes on the verge of combusting. I mentally prepare myself for the interrogation. Surely, she must know something, or why would she be here?

"Let's cut to the chase." She fires up a cigarette, something which is legal indoors in Paris, although not something I usually welcome inside my office. "I know you're my husband's mistress. I've known this for quite some time."

Her stare is anything but angry but rather composed, which is strangely odd for someone who just questioned me about being her husband's mistress. I remain quiet, not wanting to admit the truth if this is some sort of setup, but ensure my facial expression is blank with no emotion.

"I think you're a perfect companion for him. As you know, I live quite a busy life and can't always attend to his needs."

"Allegra," I begin, distancing myself across the room. "What are you trying to say?"

"I believe Dominic has developed feelings for you. I can see how he has changed. As you may or may not know, our marriage was somewhat agreed upon to help his business. So, I have a proposition for you. I'll continue to give you my blessing to have a relationship with my husband and allow him to spend more time here to fulfill your needs. But I must remain married to him, for legal purposes. Should Dominic and I end our marriage, he'll lose everything, and my reputation will be ruined."

My arms move on their own accord, crossing against my chest while my eyes narrow with a hard expression. Beneath the green silk blouse I'm wearing, my blood pressure soars, stirring up anger from behind the walls I've purposely built.

"I want to be clear in exactly why you came here," I concede, trying to understand her proposition. "Dominic must remain married to you, but you don't care that he sleeps with someone else?"

"Mi amore, us Italians believe that love can be expressed in many ways. My husband has needs, I have needs, and sometimes those needs are met by other people."

The more she speaks, the more I'm convinced she's setting me up. She stands, swinging her purse in her hands like she strolled into my office for a friendly chat. "It was nice to finally speak to you in person. Please have a think about what I've said. Have a good day, Kate."

The second she leaves my office, I let out the breath I didn't realize I'd been holding. I refrain from calling Dominic, wondering how much he knows of her impending visit. If he knows, the asshole should've warned me.

I stand at the window and stare into the city.

My phone begins to ring with the name Noah flashing across the screen. I hit accept and place him on speaker.

"What's with your timing?"

"Why? You naked in the shower?"

"Funny. I'm at work and..." I'm not sure why I hesitate. Every time the topic of Dominic comes up, Noah gets all territorial. "It's been a long day."

"Better a long day, then a long life." He sighs.

"Oh, stop being dramatic," I call him out. "And you rang because?"

"Can't an old friend ring to make sure another friend is behaving?"

I purse my lips. "I'm always behaving. It's Friday, what are your plans for tonight?"

The silence carries over the speaker. "I have to meet Morgan."

"Oh..." I mouth, unsure why this tiny stab went straight to my heart causing me to stutter. "Is everything okay?"

"Who knows with her," he grumbles with resentment. "One minute she's civil, and the next we're in a screaming match."

I hold back my words, listening to him but unsure of what to say. Women are a peculiar species, many wear their heart on their sleeve. Morgan seems no different, and she does have a daughter with him who she loves.

"There's one thing I've learned at the top, despite knowing that the other party can be irrational, you have the power to set the tone. You can control the people around you by being calm. Tonight might be good, or it might be bad."

"Why are you so wise after a shitty day? What happened, anyway?"

I can't tell him, the humiliation will leave me scarred. And why does he have to know? I haven't spoken to Dominic since last week at the bar. For now, our communication is non-existent.

But then I remember Noah is only my friend, and perhaps, a male perspective wouldn't be so bad.

"Noah," I say his name with trepidation, trying to hold back, but something tells me to be honest. "Allegra was in my office minutes before you called."

"You're fucking with me? What the hell for?"

I draw in a breath, knowing this conversation could go two ways. "In a nutshell, she told me she knows about Dominic and me. Basically, she knows that Dominic has feelings, and she won't stand in the way of us being together, but she needs to stay married to him."

The more I speak, the more I sound like a complete fool. This entire situation is the complicated mess I've been trying to avoid.

"Back the hell up," he berates with an angered tone. "She wants you to be his mistress or whatever the fuck you want to call it?"

"In layman's terms, yes."

"And so, he loves you? Is that what you're trying to tell me?"

"I never said love, Noah," I correct him. "I said feelings, emotions."

"Do you love him?"

I hesitate, but only just. "No."

"You hesitated..."

"I hesitated because you caught me off-guard with your question."

The toxic silence between us rears its ugly head. Why did I think this conversation would go well? The same argument could've been had with Charlie.

"Listen, I better go," he mumbles. "I don't blame him, Kate. Just so you know."

The call ends abruptly, forcing me to stare at the screen. His final words leave a heavier note, but Noah has often expressed his emotions, and I never read any more into it.

Instead of leaving the office, I purposely bury my head into more work, leaving just before nine. By the time I stop to grab something to eat, it's dark when I reach my apartment.

Upon opening the door and kicking off my shoes, the sound of silence welcomes the loneliness. A shower or bath will normally relax my tense muscles, but even the thought brings little solace.

Still in my work attire, I sit on the couch and turn on the television. I mindlessly channel surf to no avail until I turn the damn thing off. Frustrated with my mind unable to switch off, I open the doors to the balcony and step out into the summer's night air. The breeze is refreshing against my skin, the sounds of noise on the street drown out the silence in my head. People are walking together, laughing, and some more intimate, holding hands. The restaurant across the street is busy with lots of patrons dining out.

Last weekend feels like a lifetime ago. Perhaps there's truth to what Charlie said, Paris is beautiful, but home is where the heart is loved.

I pull my phone out of my pocket, sending Noah a quick text asking if he can talk. He responds with a simple yes. My fingers move quickly and dial his number, placing him on speaker as I lean against the window and stare into the sky.

"Hello," is all he answers, his tone flat and uninviting.

"Noah, I don't like the way we ended things tonight. I'm sorry I told you, or perhaps not sorry I told you, but sorry I didn't communicate the actual conversation correctly. But I'm calling just to make sure you're okay after meeting with Morgan."

"Sure, I guess."

His closed answers are frustrating, and my mind begins to conjure up thoughts. Does she want to reunite? Did something happen? Thoughts are rampant doing nothing to ease the tension.

"And? What happened?"

"She's seeing someone."

"Oh," I answer, not expecting that response. The more it sinks in, the more I realize his somber mood is from jealousy. *Of course, he's upset, he still loves her, right?* "I understand, Noah. You love her, and now there's someone else."

"No, Kate, you don't understand," he almost threatens me.

"Well, then enlighten me?"

"I'm not upset because she's seeing someone. I'm upset because for every second she speaks to me telling me that she's seeing some guy and wants Jessa to meet him, all my mind can think about is you and Dominic."

"Noah," I stutter, confused by why his thoughts are misplaced. "There's nothing going on right now."

"Right now." He laughs rudely.

"Why are you hell-bent on thinking I'm lying?"

"Because you hesitate every fucking time!"

"I hesitate because you're sensitive, or should I say temperamental when this subject is raised."

"And have you ever stopped to wonder why?"

I shake my head, though he can't see me. He's forcing me to look deep inside rather than scrape the surface, and the last time I did that, hearts were broken, specifically mine.

"Don't do this, Noah," I whisper. "Don't go ruining what we have."

"Because you love him? Are you thinking about taking Allegra up on her offer? Be the mistress on the side? Chances are, there's more than one of you. Why not make it a gangbang? Then he'll start charging people to come watch," he muses bitterly.

"No, Noah. I don't love him. That's all you need to know."

"And that's supposed to make me feel better? You don't love him, but you're still willing to fuck him?"

The advice I offered Noah only hours ago seems impossible to follow, controlling the people around you by how you react. My anger is stirring up within me at the choice of his words. But if I feed into his jealously and frustration, I'll be a plain old hypocrite. This is what we do, we argue, we hang up, then we bury it until it becomes a bigger problem.

But not this time. I don't want to fall back into the same bad habit when deep, down inside, I know Noah has many things on his mind. I just shouldn't be one of them.

"I understand you have a lot of things—"

"No, don't do that. Try to tell me I don't feel the way I feel."

"Noah," I bow my head trying to push away the feeling

of his subtle hints at something else. "Please don't say how you feel."

"And why shouldn't I?"

"Because if you say how you feel, it'll all change. Me, you, us..."

The quietness between us grows deeper, pure in its form while creating a blank canvas for our thoughts. Just when I think he'll hang up without a goodbye, his breathing falters the same time my heart skips a beat.

"It should've been you, Kate," he whispers. "All along... it should have been you."

FOURTEEN

NOAH

My gaze drifts toward my little girl asleep in her bed.

The sound of her tiny snores is more like long-winded breaths as innocent as the one proceeding.

My feet move as quietly as possible to adjust her yellow blanket, which is teetering on the railing of her bed. She can't go anywhere without it. According to experts, it's a habit needing to be stopped at her age. But who gives a goddamn fuck? If it makes her happy and comforts her, then let her be.

Laying in her arms is Mr. Foxy, her favorite stuffed toy. My fingers gently move the loose strands of hair away from her face, giving me space to plant a soft kiss on her forehead. The scent of her baby skin brings back so many memories, the milestones of her time with us replaying like a sweet melody.

Jessa doesn't deserve my mistakes.

The guilt spreads like wildfire, out of control with its ferocity. There are so many elements that started the blaze, moments which were out of my depth, so I neglected all the signs.

From the beginning, my infatuation with Morgan and her ignorant behavior years ago should've been the red flag. Still, instead, being a novice to love, I followed my heart or whatever the fuck it was because I had no clue what the hell I was doing.

Looking back and reflecting on our time together, I was addicted to the thrill of the chase. Morgan was unattainable, and I wanted to prove a point. My ego led the race, and while running toward the finish line to what I believed would be a victorious win, I slowly lost pieces of myself and became the man Morgan wanted me to be. That included letting go of certain people in my life.

We did everything by the book, or so I thought. I asked her to marry me before Jessa came along. The sanctity of marriage seemed important if we were going to raise a family together.

Yet, the rings on our fingers only added to the pressure of our daily lives. Our sexual connection dissipated, replaced by angry threats and resentment toward each other. I envisioned a wife, a mother, who would put her children first, not her Hollywood movie star of a sister. The more we fought, the clearer it became that we'd made a mistake fast-tracking our relationship. We never took the time to build a solid foundation, letting lust overshadow the vital elements to sustaining a long-lasting future.

And while regret plays a massive part in my conflicted emotions toward Morgan, I'm then torn every second I stare into the eyes of this beautiful child we created. I still recall the moment she was born, how nothing else in my life made me complete. How I vowed to be her father, a protector, a man she could always rely on. My own father's absence made me all the more aware of the role I needed to fulfill in my daughter's life.

But now, the one paying the highest price is Jessa. Her world has been torn apart, much of that my fault for allowing Morgan's controlling nature over our marriage to push me over the edge and into a bigger mistake. The pain was insurmountable, staring at the divorce papers on Christmas Eve. I was alone, left wondering precisely what I'd done wrong or why my child deserved a broken home. The threat of losing Jessa and being alone consumed me and drove me to the pits of darkness with only one way out.

I needed anything to take my mind off it, anything to make me forget my whole world was being taken away from me.

And then came Olivia Hawkins.

I remembered her from our childhood, and the uncanny timing gave it all the more reason as to why we both ended up in the hotel room that night. We were both bleeding from freshly opened but different wounds and the pain of losing someone.

It was supposed to be one night—all sex, no attachment, just the desperate need to control my life inside that hotel room. I wasn't doing anything wrong. As far as I was concerned, Morgan and I were separated with divorce papers making it even more official.

But the moment after, I realized the biggest mistake I made wasn't fighting for what Jessa needed. She deserved for her family to stay together, and so, if it meant that I'd give up my beliefs and become the man Morgan needed me to be, then I would.

I still remember the night like it was yesterday.

. . .

"Daddy, come say night-night."

Jessa stood at the top of the stairs, carrying her yellow blanket with bears all over it, the same blanket she dragged across the floor everywhere she went. In her other hand, she held a small stuffed brown fox. It was soft and had these big eyes like it was out of a cartoon, a last-minute purchase when I left Chicago airport three months ago.

I quickly made my way up the stairs, scooped her up in my arms, and balanced the weight of her body and the extra items she carried. Walking toward her room, I saw the night-light was already on, and her favorite book sat on top of her pillow.

"Daddy, you read to me? Puh-lease?"

I gently placed her down, tucked her in as she got comfortable, and she placed her thumb inside her mouth. As I softly read to her, her eyes began to droop, her long lashes touching her face until her soft snore echoed in the room. I leaned in, kissed her forehead before shutting the door.

The lights were dimmed downstairs in the den, the fireplace running on this rare chilly night.

"Laptop away," I scolded Morgan.

Morgan was still wearing her work clothes, giving me another excuse, some important email that had to go out right now. "Just one more—"

"Morgan," I reminded her gently. "C'mon, our therapist said we need to make time for each other when Jessa is asleep."

She nodded in agreement and shut her laptop with a sigh. "You're right. Of course. Cheese and wine?"

"How about you naked?" I pulled her body into mine and watched her giggle in my embrace.

"How about I slip into something more comfortable?" she teased.

"How about you slip into nothing?"

She leaned in, kissed my lips, instantly turning me on. I rubbed my body against hers and slid my hand beneath her skirt and along her thighs.

"I'll be back. Behave."

She walked out of the room, dropped her heels to the floor, and untucked her blouse as she went. I sat back, a smile on my face as I thought about how lucky we were to be back to where we started—a family.

I had one last chance to save us, and the second that Olivia left my hotel room, I made the call. I saved my marriage.

It was all because of that one night.

It was because of Olivia. The way she allowed me to feel like a man. That's when I decided to fight for what I wanted —my wife and kid. Perhaps it was Olivia's raw innocence that made me fight for the overbearing, stubborn woman who committed to me for life.

It was a reminder that I couldn't go back to the days of being single, where I'd aimlessly sleep with woman after woman. I fell in love with Morgan Bentley and made her my wife. In turn, she made me a father. Giving up was no longer an option.

I sat back, waiting for Morgan, busying myself by checking the latest scores when a text came in. The name popped up—Milkshake Bitch—a joke between Olivia and me from our childhood.

Unable to hide the smile that played on my lips, I read the text, and as each word registered, and I pieced it together, my throat curled into a tight ball. The bile rose so fast, I was unable to breathe in any way, shape, or form.

Two words flashed on the screen.

I'm pregnant.

. . .

I'd fucked up, and there was no turning back. When it came to telling Morgan, her reaction was warranted. She called me hurtful names and threw my clothes out on the lawn. She threatened me with legal action to gain sole custody of Jessa.

Charlie stepped in, giving me a temporary roof over my head while I tried to come to terms with it. She also reassured me that she'd do everything in her power to represent me in court, so both Morgan and I had joint custody, which seemed fair.

But Morgan is anything but a fair woman. The last few months have been hell between us, her true colors coming to light. Only in recent weeks has she settled enough that we can civilly talk about Jessa. We agreed to certain days as to when she'll stay with each parent, which forced me to find a place to live so Jessa would feel settled. We untied our assets, and fortunately for me, I still had other properties in my name, which funded my new purchase in Malibu. Jessa loves the beach, so it seemed like the perfect place for her to stay with me.

To add to the complication, I had the situation with Olivia. From the beginning, she wanted nothing from me, offering to raise the baby alone. It seemed like the only option, given that my life, including Jessa and work, is all in LA.

I've been floating in unknown waters without a life jacket to save me from imminent drowning. The only help I have willingly accepted is from Charlie. Being a lawyer specializing in family law, she's seen it all. She suggested that we don't commit to any agreements until the baby was born. Things will likely change, and my involvement in this baby's life will become more evident as time goes on.

At least, Olivia, unlike Morgan, was rational in this respect.

Closing the door behind me, my hand rests on the doorknob with a heavy heart. And then, the whispers come back to remind me that someone else can't escape me.

My hand slides into the pocket of my pants to retrieve my phone, and like I'd done so many times today, I open my photos to the one which has taunted me since Saturday night.

The simple picture was taken on the dance floor, drunk on expensive champagne and scotch. A selfie with Kate's lips pressed against my cheek mid-laugh, and my face lit up with sheer joy. We laughed until our stomachs writhed in pain, and tears rolled down our cheeks while we barely were able to stand, let alone dance.

The simple moment between us is what I have been missing all along. I knew this the moment I laid eyes on Kate.

But this isn't a simple equation. I've hurt her, abandoned our friendship, and now I have the excess baggage of children, which no woman wants from a man she's seeing.

I stare at the image numerous times, willing this feeling of yearning to stop. But as the days pass with the distance between us, an entire ocean apart, it all becomes harder to control this urge consuming me.

I make my way to the kitchen, sitting on the stool as Morgan stands across from me, scraping her hands through her hair. She's still dressed in her work clothes, and despite my intolerance toward her, Morgan will always be a beautiful woman. Though of late, I notice her dresses have been more revealing and tighter. She's also lost weight, but our relationship is strained, so I keep all of the observations to myself. We are no longer friends, only two people trying to navigate this co-parenting thing. It's a shame she has to be such a bitch about it.

"How was your trip to Paris?" she asks, rubbing her palms together nervously.

"Fine."

Unable to look me in the eye, she drops her head and crosses her arms, only to uncross them moments later. Surprisingly, when I initially told her about my trip, I expected her to lecture me on abandoning our daughter, but it never came. Her mood swings are tiresome, and I have no energy to argue with her again tonight, which is where I expect to head in a matter of minutes.

The fact is—my mind is a fucking mess after my call with Kate.

"What do you want to discuss?" I question, impatiently.

"I need you to please keep an open mind, or shall I say, I don't want to argue."

The moment she says that, alarm bells rise. "What's wrong?"

"I'm seeing someone."

I lower my head, staring at the marble countertop. This moment was bound to come, and while my anger on the subject is a given, it becomes misplaced—the conversation with Kate comes roaring back to life. I should've sucker-punched the fucker the moment I saw him at the ball, but Lex warned me to keep my peace, knowing all too well my feelings on his so-called existence.

"His name is Callum. He's a director. I just thought you should know."

Silence stirs inside of me as my stark white knuckles graze against the marble. My pulse is racing at record speed, intensifying the heat of my skin beneath my collared shirt. Morgan makes a sound with her throat, waiting for my response with bated breath.

What the fuck am I supposed to say? Congratulations, you're fucking someone else? I don't care what she does as long as my daughter is safe. Good luck to the dick who gets to call you his. I'm sure he'll have fun losing his balls to a bitch like you.

This anger is consuming me at warp speed, a typhoon unable to escape. Morgan is saying something about how she met him or where he lives, but the sound of her voice fades into the distance. The only thing I can hear is Kate's voice telling me that Dominic loves her, and his wife is fine with her being his fuck toy on the side.

I begged myself to calm down when I figured out they were still fucking each other. Then, after our weekend together, and seeing him laced with jealousy at the ball, I knew it wouldn't be long before he tried to summon her back.

He texted, he called—all the while she was with me. I lost my patience that night, our heated discussion sending her running to him, or so I thought. She promised me nothing happened, and it's taken every fiber in my being to trust her. Kate has always known her worth. It's what I've always admired about her.

But even I'll admit, I'm barely hanging on by a thread. Zero control and the seed of jealousy plant into the pit of my soul. She's so far away. I can't even see her or tell her how I really feel.

"Does he know you have kids?" I blurt out, unapologetically.

"Yes, he knows about Michael. In fact, he has met Michael along with Wyatt. I'd really like him to meet Jessa."

My head jerks up, rage pulsing through my veins. "So what? He can replace me as her dad?"

"Noah, that's not what... you know what? I knew your jealousy would get the better of you. We're over. You made sure of that the moment you fucked some whore of a stewardess," she concedes in anger.

"No, Morgan, you made sure of that the moment you sent me divorce papers. All you've done is blame me like this is all *my* fault. Well, guess what? We both fucked up our marriage. And the only one who will truly suffer is Jessa. So, the answer is no, he can't fucking meet my daughter."

"Don't threaten me, Noah," she charges, her face reddening. "If you want to play nasty, then so will I."

"It's nothing new. You've been doing it our whole marriage."

She directs her cold eyes at me. "Leave my house now. You'll see Jessa when I say so."

"You have no right holding my daughter back from me!" I jump off the stool while banging my fist on the countertop. "I don't care who you fuck or spread your legs for. I don't care if you fuck a whole army, she's my daughter, and I'll see her when I damn well please."

I grab my keys, leaving Morgan in the kitchen, and slam the door behind me.

Inside my car, I roar the engine, speeding to Charlie's place with my windows wide open and music blaring to drown out Morgan's threat. When I reach their house, my Bluetooth rings, and I see Kate's number appear, answering with a blunt hello.

"Noah, I don't like the way we ended things tonight. I'm sorry I told you, or perhaps not sorry I told you, but sorry I didn't communicate the actual conversation correctly. But

I'm calling just to make sure you're okay after meeting with Morgan," she offers, her tone genuine and non-argumentative.

"Sure, I guess," I respond flatly.

"And? What happened?"

I pinch the bridge of my nose, willing the anger to calm the fuck down. "She's seeing someone."

"Oh." Her voice softens, instantly soothing me. "I understand, Noah. You love her, and now there's someone else."

My anger comes back two-fold when I tell her she can't possibly understand. How can I look at my child and love her with all my being but regret the fact that I chose Morgan over someone who meant so much more to me years ago?

I fucked up. I let go of my best friend, and my stupid heart knows exactly that.

"Well, then enlighten me?" she answers, rudely.

I couldn't hold back any longer, telling her exactly how I felt and how she consumed my thoughts.

"Noah," she stutters as the ache spreads through me by the simple gesture of saying my name. "Nothing is going on right now."

She's still fucking him. I can hear it every time she hesitates.

"Right now." I laugh to numb the pain.

"Why are you hell-bent on thinking I'm lying?" she questions angrily.

"Because you hesitate every fucking time!" I slam my fist on the steering wheel, willing this vicious cycle to stop.

"I hesitate because you're sensitive or, should I say, temperamental when this subject is raised."

"And have you ever stopped to wonder why?" I beg.

"Don't do this, Noah," she whispers, barely audible. "Don't go ruining what we have."

"Because you love him? Are you thinking about taking Allegra up on her offer? Be the mistress on the side? Chances are, there's more than one of you. Why not make it a gangbang? Then he'll start charging people to come watch."

"No, Noah. I don't love him," she says, calmly and not feeding into my anger. "That's all you need to know."

"And that's supposed to make me feel better? You don't love him, but you're still willing to fuck him?"

"I understand you have a lot of things—"

"No, don't do that," I yell, berating her for her ability to fuck with my mind. "Don't try to tell me I don't feel the way I feel."

"Noah..." she trails off. "Please don't say how you feel."

"And why shouldn't I?"

"Because if you say how you feel, it'll all change. Me, you, us..."

The silence falls upon us, and I close my eyes because it's now or never.

"It should've been you, Kate," I whisper, shaking my head with my eyes closed. "All along, it should have been you."

Her breathing is loud enough to be heard over the speaker. "You don't know what you're asking of me. I need to go."

"Kate, stop. I'm sorry. I'm angry, okay, but I mean what I said."

"I heard you, Noah," she announces, then pausing. "I promise I heard you."

The call ends abruptly, leaving the line completely

dead. I've pushed Kate, throwing caution to the wind and giving her all of me, only for her to walk away.

No sentiment in return, no admission.

I give myself ten minutes to compose myself before entering Charlie and Lex's place to see Eric at the table talking animatedly with Charlie.

"Is everything okay?" Charlie asks, concerned. "You look..."

"Like my asshole after rough penetration," Eric says bluntly.

"Thank you," I answer sarcastically, then walk toward the fridge, grabbing a beer. "I'm sure Morgan's lawyer will be calling you on Monday to seek full custody of Jessa."

"Jesus Christ, Noah. What happened?"

"Tomorrow," is all I say. "I really don't want to talk about this now. Talk about anything else, even Eric's asshole for all I care."

Eric pulls his face back in shock until he's distracted by his phone. "Like seriously, what's up with the universe?"

"Now, what's wrong?" Charlie moans.

"It's weird, just my brother texting me all of a sudden. Well, not all of a sudden but like the past week. He's nice, and I don't know... he's opening up about shit, which is weird as fuck because we never ever talk."

Charlie glances my way, forcing me to drink more to control my anger toward his brother.

"What do I possibly have that he wants?"

"I don't know," Charlie mumbles. "Did I tell you we saw him in Versailles?"

"Yes, after he told me. And check this out, you'll love this, Noah. He asked me what the situation is between you and Kate? It's just bizarre."

Suddenly, my curiosity piques. "What did you tell him?"

"Nothing, really. You used to be friends, maybe you guys fucked in Paris, but no one is telling me anything," Eric answers with a sarcastic tone.

"We didn't fuck in Paris, okay?"

"Really?" Charlie raises her brow while leaning back in her chair. "I could've sworn—"

"No," I say firmly. "We aren't like that. Listen, I need to speak to Lex. Is he around?"

Charlie sighs. "Where do you think he is?"

I head toward Lex's office, eager to leave Eric and his troubles. Noticing the door slightly open, I knock before entering, Lex welcoming me in. Taking a seat in the brown leather chair, my fingers skim the tip of the beer bottle in my hand.

"Rough night?"

"Morgan's seeing someone else."

Lex nods his head, resting back in his chair. "I understand. It hurts. Bound to happen, though."

I bow my head, running my hands through my hair. "That's the thing. It doesn't hurt."

"I see," Lex simply states. "Does it have something to do with a certain someone in Paris?"

"I don't know where my head is at," I tell him openly. "I'm trying to make things right, be a good dad. My kids need me."

Lex nods. He's always been a good listener, and I respect his opinion. On the other hand, Haden would be telling me to hit the clubs and get some pussy to get over myself.

"Who am I to judge matters of the heart. Lucky for you, you missed my multiple breakdowns during operation 'let's win Charlotte back.' Kate endured it all. She saw me at my absolute worst, the only person at the time who got through to me. You know what you got to do, so just do it. No more questions."

"Yeah, Kate's good like that." I smile fondly. "The whole different continent thing doesn't help. I guess, for now, I have to park that situation. It's not like I can go back anytime soon, and she has a job she can't exactly leave."

"You know what you want, don't let anyone else stop you from getting just that," he says, wisely.

I nod my head in agreement. Although Lex is married to Charlie, I consider him like an older brother. He just understands me and never judges my poor life decisions.

"Are you really working? Or in here escaping Eric?"

Lex chuckles. "A bit of both. So, have you thought more about the offer?"

For the last two years, I've worked on some side projects with Lex. As much as I enjoy working for Lantern Publishing, I've outgrown the role as West Coast Operations Manager.

"I have, and it's a great opportunity."

"But?"

"No buts. I'm concerned about leaving Haden short, especially since we have a massive increase in sales, and demand is outweighing supply right now."

"Listen, leave Haden and Lantern Publishing to me, we'll find a suitable replacement. You have proven yourself no matter what has been thrown at you. I have trust that you can drive this sector of Lexed"

The respect of Lex isn't something anyone should take for granted. He's a mogul, a self-made billionaire.

"I'll get my lawyer on the contract," I joke.

"Your lawyer helped me draw up the contract," he admits, openly. "If I'm low-balling you, blame her."

This opportunity is more than just a job offer. It would set me up for life. Although I'm financially comfortable having kept my condo back in Boston and another in downtown LA, my new place in Malibu set me back. The divorce with Morgan isn't finalized with some loose matters still pending, and it won't surprise me if she tries to ask for alimony.

"So, is that a yes?"

I extend my hand to shake on it.

"Welcome to the team, Noah."

Lex pulls out the Macallan as we toast to the news before going over some details. Throwing my head into work is a stress reliever until Charlie walks in and makes herself comfortable on Lex's lap. Those two don't bother me as much anymore. I've learned to shut out their romantic behavior in my presence as long as clothes remain on and hands are in full view.

"I'm assuming congratulations are in order?" Charlie grins, knowingly.

"It'll be some challenge."

"Since when have you ever backed down from a challenge? Remember when we were kids, and I'd set up all these stunts in our backyard like jumping off the tree onto the trampoline? And whoever did it in the quickest time won?"

"I remember," I scoff, rolling my eyes. "It cost me a fractured wrist."

"Sorry about that."

"Thank God I was a kid. Could've been detrimental as an adult."

"Ew, gross." Charlie drags while cringing. "Anyway, back there, in the kitchen, was that true? About Kate?"

"Why would I lie?"

Charlie eyes me the same time Lex raises his brow.

"Apparently, Dominic is besties with Eric all of sudden and asked about Noah and Kate, specifically if they've been intimate," Charlie tells Lex.

"So basically, he is asking if you are fucking because the prick's jealous?" Lex asserts, keeping his expression blank.

I purse my lips, keeping my mouth shut.

"Why do men have to be so frustrating," Charlie complains, throwing her hands in the air. "Just say how you feel, get over yourself, and it doesn't matter whether another man is jealous or not. If it's you she wants, then that's all that matters."

"You're her best friend, you tell me?"

"When it comes to the subject of you, dear cousin, Kate is a very closed book."

"It's not as simple as you make it out to be," I quickly interject. "For starters, we have a geographical issue."

"So? Lex lived in London when we reunited."

"True," Lex agrees. "I'd have gone anywhere to be with you, no questions asked."

Charlie pouts, lovingly wrapping her arms around Lex's neck. "Aw... baby."

"Okay, you two are making me sick. But seriously, it's all too complicated right now. I need time to think."

"Then think, but if I were you, I wouldn't leave it too long, especially when someone else is desperate to get his hands on her."

"You just said it doesn't matter?" I almost shout at Charlie. "If she wants me, that's all that matters."

"Yeah, it's probably wise not to listen to me," Charlie

ponders while creasing her brows. "Eric makes daiquiris with way too much rum. I couldn't even walk straight to this room."

"So basically, your advice is fruitless? Nice one. Listen, I'm going to head home."

"Why don't you crash here? You shouldn't be alone," Charlie offers.

"I'd rather be alone than in a house where you're drunk, probably ready to maul your husband. It's been nice knowing you."

I wave goodbye, leaving the room as Charlie giggles, knowing I made the right decision. The two of them are so annoying yet deep inside, they remind me a lot of Kate and me.

On the ride back home, I think about calling Kate but know we both need time to process. I have to get my act together, and pushing her could be detrimental. She's my best friend, someone I know very well. Right now, she's trying to ignore everything I said because she hates relinquishing control. She's the female Lex, which is why she holds such a powerful position, and nobody messes with her.

But I also know she's incredibly lonely in Paris, despite her reluctance to admit it. And anything romantic is a trigger for her. She's been scarred multiple times, and when it comes to matters of the heart, the wall she's purposely built around her will stand tall, ready for any attack.

I don't want her to lose again. Not now, not ever.

Because as much as I beg myself not to admit it, throwing the thought into a dungeon with no key or chance of escape, I'm falling in love with her.

Again.

Or maybe, I never stopped loving her.

FIFTEEN

KATE

If you stare at the ceiling long enough, your imagination can visualize anything.

I see a beach, waves crashing against the shore with a beautiful sunset setting on the horizon. Then a sprawling countryside, lusciously green, accompanied by the sounds of crickets and other insects basking in the sunlight.

Then my mind switches to chaos—a circle full of animals, loud noises, claps, and cheering with boisterous music and the roar of a lion. More bright colors, fire, complete and utter nonsense.

I haven't slept.

Turning to my side with my head resting on my hands, the sun begins to rise outside my bedroom window, and just like that, morning is upon us.

My phone call to Noah last night was more than just a phone call to make sure he was okay. It changed everything between us.

Or maybe, just maybe, I've been blind to see it wasn't

just that phone call. It has been a series of events leading to that moment.

I hung up out of fear, pushing him away because I don't know how to handle my emotions. The lack of control in my life is something I struggle with. I've never had to factor in anyone else besides myself, and I know myself pretty well. Therefore, life has become somewhat easy to navigate through.

But then he said it should've been me.

I tried to picture it, the two of us together four years ago. No matter how I twisted it in my mind, it didn't fit. We were the best of friends, but being lovers is something I can't envision. The more I dwell on it, the more I believe he was just hurting, and me being back in his life confused his feelings.

I fell asleep to the sound of traffic, only to wake up a few hours later to the obnoxious toot of a horn. I've missed my Saturday yoga class and bypassed my early-morning stroll to the café for coffee and breakfast. Everything is out of whack, and no matter how hard I try, I can't get him out of my mind.

Spending my Saturday inside the office was my only ticket out of this mess. With my head buried in a forecasting spreadsheet after firing off a dozen emails warning my workers to get their shit together and stop making errors, the sound of my phone startles me.

"Working on a Saturday?" Lex greets, sounding relaxed. "The model employee."

"I needed to clear my head."

"I see," he simply says. "I've read your emails, quite the aggressive tone today, Miss Hamilton. Is everything okay?"

Although Lex is technically my boss, our friendship is what makes our union strong. I respect his opinion, given his ability to remove emotion from a situation and think rationally.

"Lex, can I ask you something?"

"You know you can ask me anything."

"It's about Noah."

"I figured as much."

"Wait, you did?"

"If I'm being honest, yes."

I fall silent, unsure how to ask the question on the tip of my tongue. "How much do you know?"

"I know enough."

"Oh..."

"Is that your question?"

I wanted to ask more, but all of a sudden, involving Lex seems inappropriate. I don't want to muddle their bro code nor come off like some needy woman.

"Do you want my perspective?" he asks, then continues, "Though you may not like it."

"You know I've always respected your opinion."

"Noah is different around you. Life has been injected back into him. He has done it tough the last few years, and last weekend proved what was missing in his life."

"What's that?"

"*You.*"

The simple word holds so much weight, the weight tugging me in all different directions and causing my inability to sleep or function as a normal human being.

"Lex, it's not that simple."

"Do you know what the problem is? You're always in control of your life. And now you are powerless. I understand exactly how that feels. But good things can come from us letting go."

"Everything in my life will change..." I trail off, closing

my eyes to gather my thoughts. "It just wouldn't work. He has his life, and I have mine."

"Take it from me, overthinking is the devil's playground. There are some things in life where natural progression is inevitable, and falling in love with someone is one of those things."

"I never said I was falling in love with Noah," I defend openly.

"You didn't have to, Kate. I am a keen observer. It's why I'm a billionaire."

I laugh softly. "I forgot about that."

"Why don't you fly out next weekend for Amelia's birthday? I insist you stay with us. Make it a week so you can catch up with Charlotte and the girls. Javier can cover the office while you're gone."

"Amelia's birthday, right," I say with a heavy sigh. "I'd love to, but these contracts—"

"It's not a suggestion but rather a demand," he states firmly. "Remember who's the boss?"

"Fine," I tell him. "But I'm warning you... I'm this close to complaining to HR about your attitude."

Lex chuckles, easing my worry. "It'll be good to have you back home."

Home—there's that word again.

Our conversation shifts to work as it always does with us. Lex strongly suggests I call it a day and go out to unwind before I end up firing my entire team. He isn't entirely wrong. I've had enough of incompetence, and today is the wrong day to fuck up under my watch.

Emile, my personal assistant, joins me for a late dinner at a small restaurant near the office. The chef is known for his stunning good looks and ability to make any cuisine taste perfect. We order the expensive champagne, laughing as we drink and eat ourselves into a stupor.

"What are we celebrating?"

"Life," I announce, holding my glass in the air. "No celebrating, just Lex's orders to go unwind."

"It's been crazy the last week. I didn't get a chance to ask you how last weekend was?"

"Where do I begin..."

Four glasses later, I spilled the entire beans, including my affair with Dominic. It felt good to get it all out, though Emile is stunned at my admission, her big blue eyes becoming wider with curiosity the more I speak.

"Okay, so let's start with Dominic. What are you going to do?"

"Nothing. There's nothing to do. I'm not going to be his mistress because Allegra wants me to be. It's complicated, and it's not really what I want anymore..."

"You want Noah?"

"I don't know what I want. I know that when Dominic and I were doing what we did, I felt powerful. He made me feel like a woman," I say with honesty, knowing the glasses of champagne have something to do with it. "But when I'm with Noah... it's just..."

"*Parfaite?*" She smiles while tossing her long chocolate-brown hair to the side.

"Not exactly perfect. We argue a lot." I grin fondly. "But there's just something between us I can't explain. He makes me feel safe, but he understands my passions. I'm not a toy to him, nor a mistress..."

Emile leans forward, placing her hand on mine. Her fingers are adorned with rings and her nails perfectly mani-cured. "There's a saying in French, *Entre deux cœurs qui s'aiment, nul besoin de paroles.*"

"Between two hearts that love each other, no need for words," I repeat, letting out a sigh. "Love is a strong word."

"*Oui,*" she says, her gaze fixated on mine. "Don't let it slip away because you're scared. This could be a good thing, Kate. This could be the moment that changes your soul forever."

~

Charlie's black SUV pulls up along the curb, followed by an excited wave. I hate LAX with a passion. The traffic jam of cars to the impatient people pushing through and knocking you with their suitcases. It's been three years since I last stepped foot in California, and boy, do the awful memories come crashing like a tidal wave.

"How was the flight?" Charlie asks after loading my things into the car and giving me a tight hug.

"Exhausting."

"You better find some energy because I've got three girls at home dying to suck the rest of your life away."

Charlie isn't exaggerating. The girls are nonstop. They have to show me everything under the sun, and on occasion, I get an "Aunty Kate, watch me!" only to watch Ava do some random jump or hop. I have no clue how both Lex and Charlie do it full-time. I'm utterly exhausted in their presence.

By dinner, I can see their faces grow tired. Amelia wants to stay up to finish watching some television show which Charlie agrees to while Lex sorts out Ava and Addison for bed.

I check my phone for what feels like the millionth time today. Still, nothing from Noah, assuming Charlie or Lex told him I was coming. I equally play my stubborn part, not contacting him because, frankly, I don't know what to say or even how I feel. After my dinner with Emile, I thought my sentiments came out clearer. It turns out, when the champagne wore off, I was back to square one of feeling confused.

"You know, he's home if you want to see him?" Charlie raises her eyes to meet mine.

"See who?"

Charlie's smile fades from wary to pensive. "Noah. He texted me about some movie, asking me if it was a chick flick."

"Oh... does he live far from here?"

"About fifteen minutes, I can give you his address?"

"No." I grimace hopelessly. "I'm good."

We work silently at the kitchen table putting party favors together until the pressure mounts, frustration seeps into every crevice, and I can't take it anymore. I need closure, finality, something to make me sleep tonight.

"You know what? I'd like that address. If you'll excuse me, I'll be back soon."

Charlie doesn't say a word, texting me the address which appears promptly on my phone and hands me the keys to her car.

I type the address into the GPS, then remember that I'm on the other side of the road. My mind is scattered, reverting back to my English driving, giving myself a heart attack as headlights come straight at me. The road to Malibu feels longer than the fifteen minutes Charlie implied, only adding to the anxiety of it all.

The car is parked in front of his place. I hop out immediately, not giving myself time to back out, and my fist bangs on the door, louder than I should've allowed it to. Tapping my foot impatiently, I cross my arms until the lights come on. Noah opens the door dressed in his gray sweats and no shirt.

Shit—I'm screwed.

The direction of my eyes falls upon his perfectly sculpted chest to the six-pack of abs cut to perfection. Why does he have to be so sexy? Was he always like this?

"Kate?" His eyes widen in shock. "What are you doing here?"

"I wanted to talk."

"You flew over here to talk?"

"No, I flew over here for Amelia's birthday. After all, she is my goddaughter. Can I come in?"

He leans against the door in all his glory, extending his hand to welcome me in.

"Isn't it too early for gray sweatpants season?" I mumble, averting my gaze from the noticeable bulge demanding my attention. Count to ten, take deep breaths. You can get through this.

"Gray sweatpants season?"

"Never mind," I say while stepping into the foyer.

The condo is nothing short of stunning—a contemporary, modern space with floor-to-ceiling glass windows and, of course, the most breathtaking view of the ocean. It's not overly large but decorated with simple furniture creating a cozy feel.

"Nice place you have here." I draw my attention back to him, though keeping my distance. "Why did you choose Malibu?"

"I wanted something near the beach, but close to Jessa. The commute to work is painful but doable."

Inside the living room, his laptop is open to what appears to be work emails. There's a beer on the coffee table and some movie on the screen, which is paused on a shooting scene.

All of a sudden, my nerves cripple me. The air is tight, and I'm questioning why I came here. Just breathe. You can handle this.

"Noah, about our call."

"Yes?"

"You said things..."

"I did say things."

"And those things you said."

"Yes?"

"I think you're confused. There, I said it," I admit, burying my feelings deep inside. If he knew how my thoughts have drifted to something more, he could use it against me like every other man in my life. "I'm a woman, one who's in your life. We're close, and I'm glad we're close because I've missed you. But you can't go changing things on us. We're fine the way we are, and with Morgan gone, I understand it's only natural to think you have feelings for me when, in fact, maybe I'm just a rebound thought."

Noah shuffles closer to me, closing the gap between us. My heart rate spikes, creating a frenzy within me and muddling my thoughts. I blame his scent as well as his half-naked body.

"You're wrong," he breathes. "Firstly, you're not just any woman. You're Kate Hamilton, CEO of Lexed Europe. You're smart, intelligent, witty, and above all that, you're beautiful."

"A lot of women are beautiful, Noah..."

"They're not you."

His lips are inches away from mine. A kiss, if this is where it's heading, can change it all, and that alone terrifies me. We'll never be able to bounce back to just friends.

I place my hands on his chest, the instant burn inside of me becoming unbearable. I'm filled with regret for touching him, but my hands refuse to move in any other direction.

"Noah, we both need to think about this. You're not just a fling for me or a quick fuck. There's too much history between us. If I were with you, we'd be more."

"I want more."

"You don't know what you're asking..." I trail off as his lips inch closer and graze against mine until the sound of his phone ringing startles us both. Tilting his head to glance at the number, his eyes widen with curiosity.

"I'm sorry, I have to take this."

He grazes my arm before grabbing his phone and answering, giving me time to gather my thoughts and regroup.

"Is everything okay?" he answers, worried, the tone in his voice panicked. "Shit. How high? Okay, just stay calm and call 911 now. I'll try to get there soon. If I drive, it'll take me hours. I'll see if I can get a flight, okay? Bye."

"What's wrong, Noah?"

His face has drained, pacing the area in front of him in a daze. "It was Olivia. Nash has a fever, and he's stopped drinking, plus he's really restless. I don't know..."

I take a deep breath and stop him, clutching onto both his arms. "Look at me. You can do this. She needs you to be strong right now. Imagine how terrified she must be with him. Go get changed, pack a bag, and I'll get the car ready and organize you a flight."

"But work, and shit, I have to pick up Jessa for the party on Sunday."

"I'll get Charlie to sort it out, okay? Now go pack."

He disappears into the room while I pull up the airlines and find the next flight to San Francisco. After booking a flight which leaves in ninety minutes, I quickly call Charlie and explain what's happened.

"Oh my gosh. No, leave Jessa with me. I'll text Morgan now. Does Noah need anything? I'm worried about him."

"He's freaked out, of course, but I'll get him to the airport."

"Thank you, Kate. Call me when you're done, okay?"

I hang up the phone just as Noah walks out of the room in a pair of jeans, hoodie, and a duffel bag. We climb into Charlie's car and race down Pacific Coast Highway at a reasonably safe speed.

"I can't do this," he almost chokes when the airport appears in front of us. "What if we lose him? He's only ten weeks old."

"You'll do this, you know why? You have no choice. This little boy needs you. His existence isn't a mistake."

"You're the first person to say that."

"Say what?"

"That this isn't a mistake."

"A child should never be a mistake." I rest my hand on his thigh to reassure him. "Sure, perhaps the timing wasn't great, but this is what life handed you. You're a great dad to Jessa and have so much love to give to Nash even though he may not be close by."

The departure terminal is straight ahead and surprisingly quiet. With the car at a complete standstill, we both sit in silence until I find the courage to say what needs to be said, knowing what he should hear right now to give him strength.

"I'm here, Noah. Right beside you when you need me. You're not alone."

His eyes turn down, avoiding my gaze. Just one look at him, and I know he's terrified. Noah loves his daughter, and being a father is the most crucial role in his life. Now, he's faced with the unknown, of being a father to another child under different circumstances. I can see him fall into the dark place Charlie warned me about, my heart bleeding along with this. No matter the mistakes we make, we have to forgive ourselves in order to find true happiness.

Opening the door, he steps out of the car but then leans his head through the window.

"Wait for me, please."

I simply nod, though not understanding if he means now or forever.

But either way, he needs me.

I don't want to lose him, and I'll stand by his side as the friend he so desperately needs because I refuse to let him fall.

As for my own heart, I just need to let the chips fall where they may.

SIXTEEN

NOAH

I t was the moment every parent dreads—a spiked fever prompting a panicked call to the paramedics and a dash to the ER.

I stare into his little face, the face of my ten-week-old son—Nash Alexander Mason—resting in my arms while he manages to sleep without the cries of pain.

It has all been a whirlwind since the moment I stepped off the plane and headed straight for the hospital. My stomach was twisted in knots over the concern for my son and feeling completely helpless. It instills a level of fear every parent endures when their child is sick, especially an infant.

Upon arriving, Olivia is distraught, doing her best to hold it together, but I can see the exhaustion on her face from the lack of sleep to the fear over Nash's well-being. It's late, and she's in her tee and sweats with her hair in one of those messy buns. Since I saw her last, she's lost a lot of weight, the remnants of her pregnancy weight almost gone.

"Mr. and Mrs. Mason," the doctor calls as she walks into the room with her chart. "I'm Dr. Lester."

"No, he's not my husband. But that's beside the point. What's wrong with Nash?" Olivia rushes, panicked.

"Nash has an infection. We've tested a range of things, some have come back negative, and other results take longer. We'd like to monitor him overnight. If his fever drops and he continues to stay hydrated, he'll be able to go home tomorrow. Being that he's an infant, we won't be inducing any medication, hoping his body can fight it off."

"How did this happen?" I question, still rocking him in my arms.

"It could've been anywhere. Most likely, he was exposed to someone contagious."

Olivia bends her neck as her eyes glass over, and her posture falls in the tattered GAP t-shirt she's wearing. "I take him for walks and to run some errands, but that's it."

"Let's continue to observe him tonight. Both of you are welcome to stay, and I'll see you in the morning," Dr. Lester informs us before scribbling something on her chart and leaving the room.

"There was this lady at the post office. She touched his face to squeeze his cheek. It's my fault. I'm a bad mother," Olivia cries.

"You're not a bad mother," I reassure her, keeping my voice low not to wake him. "I remember when Jessa was one, we took her to the playground, and she caught chicken pox from another kid who wasn't showing signs of the virus. These things happen, but the important thing is that you followed your maternal instincts and rushed him here."

Olivia nods her head, wiping away the tears from her face.

"It's been hard, Noah. He's a fantastic sleeper during the day, but at night, he's up every four hours," she chokes, trying to compose herself. "My milk slowed down for some reason, and I've had to switch him to formula. It turns out the formula made him constipated, so then I had to try another brand."

"Why didn't you tell me all of this?" I stress, slightly irritated she's held this information from me. "I told you I want to be a part of his life as much as I can be. That means knowing his struggles or changes to his routine."

"Honestly, Noah, I didn't want to burden you."

"He's my son." My tone wavers before I clear my throat. "You're not burdening me."

Olivia raises her eyes to meet mine. "I promise to share this information, okay? I've just been tired. And work has been asking me to come back, and it's a lot of things."

"What did you tell them?"

"Nothing. I have no idea how to juggle working as an airline hostess with an infant. My hours are long, it's not a nine-to-five job, as you know. But I can't stay on leave forever. There are bills to pay. I'll have to look for something else."

"I told you I want to help, split the cost. It's the least I can do."

"I know, Noah. You just need to be patient with me. I have no clue what I'm doing, and I appreciate having you help when you can, especially because you've done this before. Speaking of which, I meant to ask you, does Morgan know about Nash?"

I nod my head, staring at Nash's little face. Although he's so young, his features have developed and look almost identical to when I was his age. At least, that's according to my mom.

"I told her. She said nothing. Actually, no, she said congratulations with a forced smile and hasn't asked about him since."

Olivia's brows draw together as her face softens. "I'm sorry."

"Don't be sorry," I remark harshly, frustrated with Morgan's attitude. "Morgan is difficult, and it's not your problem."

"Here, let me take Nash, and why don't you go get something to eat?"

I hand him over to her, the instant weight disappearing from my arms, leaving me hollow. I tell her I'll be back, walking out of the room and outside the hospital for some fresh air.

The air in San Francisco inhales much differently than LA. Cleaner, or perhaps, it's all in my imagination. With my phone in hand, I hit dial to Kate, promising I'd update her once I had some news.

"Noah, is everything okay? We're all worried here?" Kate rushes.

"An infection. They're doing some further tests and monitoring him overnight. The fever has dropped, slightly."

"I'm sorry, Noah. And you? How are you holding up?"

I can hear Charlie in the background, throwing questions at Kate. It's a distraction, and I really want to hear Kate's voice, not my cousin acting like a crazed lunatic.

"Is there somewhere you can go? So we can talk in private?"

"Of course, let me call you back."

Moments later, my phone rings. "Okay, I'm alone. Is everything okay?"

My head drops at the same time my chest tightens. The guilt is consuming me, bringing all my failures to light. I'm just like him, the father who never stepped foot in my home because he had some other life. Neither one of my kids deserve this, and that's all I am—an absent father.

"How am I supposed to do this, Kate? I can't be in two places at the same time. I know what it's like not to have a dad around. I watched my mom sacrifice her whole life for me. Is that fair to Olivia?"

"Noah," Kate breathes, calming my nerves. "You're doing the best you can, given the circumstances. Sure, the distance isn't helping. I know you have Jessa here, but have you considered asking Olivia to move closer to you?"

"No, I didn't think of asking because I know she has her own life."

"It's just a suggestion, and it doesn't hurt to ask. I'm not a parent, but from a practical standpoint, if she lived in LA, you'd have more time with your son."

"My life is a fucked-up mess."

"No one is perfect," she tries to reassure me. "This is your time right now, and you'll never get these moments back. Go spend time with your son, Noah. He needs you, and so does Olivia."

"Will you wait for me?"

"I promised I would, right?"

"Kate," I whisper, needing to say so much more. "I'll be home soon. I need to see you."

"I'm not going anywhere right now, Noah."

We hang up the phone, and with a clearer mind, I wander back to the room thinking about Kate's suggestion. It never occurred to me to ask Olivia to move because, in the back of my mind, I placed her in the same category as Morgan—a woman. Therefore, difficult and stubborn. But Olivia isn't like that, now that I think about it rationally.

Nash sleeps through the night, and by morning, his fever has dropped with his appetite returning. The doctor discharges him around midday, sending us home to continue monitoring him.

I send Kate a quick text, letting her know my plans.

Me: *I'm going to stay one more night. I just want to make sure Nash is okay.*

Kate: *Of course, it's understandable. Are you staying in a hotel?*

Me: *No, Olivia offered her couch. Will I see you tomorrow?*

The response doesn't come, the repeated checking of my phone to an empty screen. An hour later, I see it sitting there.

Kate: *I'll see you tomorrow.*

Olivia lives in a one-bedroom apartment close to the airport. It's small but has everything she needs considering she barely stays home when she's working full-time. Her job as an airline stewardess has her flying across the country, which is how we reconnected.

Inside her bedroom is Nash's crib. She places him down, informing me she'll take a shower. I settle in the living room, opening my laptop, and trying to get work done since I want to stay another night to make sure he continues to recover. But as much as I try to concentrate, my mind drifts to Kate.

Darkness falls upon us quickly as Olivia and Nash sleep soundly in the room. I bury myself in work, the only thing I can do to clear my mind. With my phone on silent, not to wake them, I now notice the five missed calls from Morgan.

In a panic, I dial her back, worried something has happened with Jessa related to the birthday party they attended today.

"What's wrong? Is Jessa okay?"

"You let me walk into Charlie's house without telling me your girlfriend would be there? Oh, sorry, is that fiancée? I'm not sure what I should call her." Morgan fumes in an arctic tone. "Imagine my surprise when I see her sitting with our daughter?"

I attempt to keep my voice down not to wake Olivia and Nash. "Morgan, what are you talking about?"

"I'm talking about Kate," she seethes, raising her voice. "You didn't even give me the respect of telling me you were fucking her!"

"We're not fucking. Will you calm down?"

"Don't you dare tell me to calm down! Is that why you went to Paris? To go chasing after the woman you've been in love with our entire marriage? Tell me, Noah, did I ever have a chance with you? Or was she always the one?"

I keep silent, no fight left in me to argue with her. When it comes to women, Morgan and Olivia are on the opposite ends of the spectrum. Olivia isn't one to argue. She's very respectful of other people and communicates without drama. Morgan, on the other hand, is an emotionally-charged woman. A goddamn bitch when she wants to be.

"I figured you'd stay silent," she sneers. "And you know what hurts the most? I did the right thing, Noah. I told you about Callum, then asked if it was okay to meet Jessa. I knew you were angry, so I gave you space to process. But you didn't care. You let her sit with my daughter like they were best friends. Not only that, she had the audacity to call my daughter a liar when I questioned her. Goddammit, Noah, I'm her mother! How dare you allow that!"

"Morgan, I've been occupied, Olivia had—"

"Don't talk to me about your personal life. I don't want to hear about you marrying Kate and playing happy family or about the other women in your life. In fact, don't talk to me. If you need to contact me, you can go through your lawyer, and don't you dare think of stepping foot in my home to see your daughter."

The line goes dead.

I bury my head in my hands, wishing this nightmare to disappear. No matter what I do, I can't gain any control in my life. And just when I admit my feelings to Kate, begging her to be honest because I can't go on living this lie like I don't feel anything, her actions cause a bigger headache in my life.

Morgan has every right to be upset because, frankly, I'd react the same way.

With exhaustion weighing heavy on my shoulders, I shut down my laptop and lay on the sofa. I often thought the world would be a better place without me in it. Each day, I'm paying for my mistakes. The challenge of recovering is becoming harder with every breath I take.

Yet from the smallest of windows, I've experienced happiness again. Kate brought all that back into my life in just one weekend. But now, the reality is coming into full vision. Kate will never understand my lifestyle and the demands of being a parent. Despite Morgan's earlier outburst, I don't blame her, but no way in hell will I allow her to gain full custody of Jessa.

And she's revealed the truth, something I've buried for years. I never forgot about Kate during my marriage. She was always there in the back of my mind, a constant comparison to Morgan. It was unfair. Perhaps Morgan is right—we never really had a chance.

It's all a fucking mess, and somehow, I need to start

cleaning it all up to avoid losing the only thing that matters to me.

My children.

SEVENTEEN

KATE

Charlie had gone all out planning Amelia's birthday party.

Amelia is anything but the traditional girl, repelling anything involving fairies, unicorns, or the color pink. Addison, the complete opposite of her older sister, is wearing a princess dress every day and demands everyone call her *Belle*. Ava, being the middle child, is a mixture of the two.

Lex and Charlie's house is sprawled across acres with views of the canyons, an expensive piece of real estate attached to a generous price tag. I still recall the day Lex put in the offer, the staggering amount he paid because, honestly, the man can do anything.

The house is decorated with a supernatural theme and a large UFO bouncy castle in the yard. There are pretend aliens scattered across the lawn, the attention to detail meticulous as they were loaned from a movie set.

We spent hours last night preparing, from favor bags to baking cookies in the shape of UFOs. Charlie insisted on handmaking everything herself aside from the cake. During the night, I wondered if Lex summoned me here to simply assist with the party's preparation. However, it did take my mind off Noah.

Outside on the patio is a long table with a green table-cloth covering it. We presented it as a grazing table, including a blob of Jell-O, which looks like a brain. It grossed me out last night, and this morning, I still felt the exact level of disgust.

"You really know how to pull off a fantastic kids' party," I praise Charlie while rearranging the platters on the table to fit more snacks for the kids. "My mother's idea of a birthday party was store-bought cake and balloons my brothers blew up only to suck the helium out of them."

"As you Brits so fondly say, I'm buggered," Charlie drags, a yawn escaping her. "And it hasn't even started."

Guests start arriving an hour later to a very excited birthday girl. The kids run straight for the UFO bouncy castle, laughter and screams suddenly echoing in the previously quiet yard.

Julian walks into the backyard along with Adriana. He's carrying a large gift with a navy bow on top, looking rather sexy in a pair of chino shorts, a black tee, and a pair of stark-white sneakers. Despite my resentment toward him years ago when he was trying to claim Charlie back, I'd be a fool to admit the man isn't handsome. He's one of those men who walk into a room, and all eyes turn to look at him. Just like Noah, Haden, and although it pains me to admit it, Lex too.

And I hate that seeing Adriana happily beside him drags to the surface my buried feelings toward Noah. I've always been the single one in the group, and it never bothered me until this very moment.

Andy is beside them, looking so much older and a spitting image of Elijah from memory. Luna, their daughter, is absolutely gorgeous with her bouncing curls and bright green eyes, dressed in a yellow tutu and running straight for the bouncy castle.

I kiss both Adriana and Julian hello as we linger on the patio.

"I've missed you," Adriana squeals by my side, wearing a maxi dress in the same shade as Luna's tutu. "Talk French to me?"

"Le français est une belle langue."

Adriana clasps her hand onto her chest. "How romantic!"

"You didn't even know what she said?" Julian teases her.

Andy appears less than amused. "Yeah, Mom, what if she said your poop smells lovely?"

Adriana rolls her eyes. "Boys... and what did you say?"

I laugh, placing my hand on her shoulder. "French is a beautiful language."

Lex walks over with his hands in his pockets, kissing his sister and extending a handshake to Julian. When it comes to Lex and Julian, their dynamic always fascinates me, since there was a time when either one would've pointed a gun in each other's temple for the love of Charlie. And though I never admitted it, a tub of popcorn was always in hand as I watched on the sideline.

Though today they appear civil as Julian asks Lex a question about a meeting he had, and Lex responds respectfully.

Rocky is also here, minus Nikki. Their son, Will, has grown so tall, a teenager now with a slight mustache and a small break of pimples scattered across his forehead. Rocky is exactly how I remember him, burly with a tight hug in tow.

"How's my favorite British bird doing?"

"I'm the only British bird you know, so, of course, I'm your favorite," I remind him with a knowing grin.

"Eric introduced me to his friend, Alistair," Rocky informs me with a shudder. "So trust me, you're not the only one."

"Ah, yes." I giggle, shaking my head at Eric's friend. "Quite the little drama queen, isn't he? So, Nikki's not with you?"

"She's back home. It's been chaos lately, and I keep telling her to hire someone else."

"Well, tell her I miss her. I haven't spoken to her in a while."

"I'll pass it on." He smiles before grabbing a plate and piling on a large amount of food.

The backyard is filled with Amelia's friends and family. Children are running around, chaos everywhere you look. I happily sat with Adriana, scanning the area and noticing Eric isn't here. I send him a text, but he doesn't respond.

I'm busily chatting with Julian about the history of the French Revolution when Morgan walks in with Jessa. My eyes gravitate toward Jessa, the little girl by her side who couldn't look any more like her daddy—mousy brown hair draping down the side of her face, identical shade to Noah's, to the hazel-colored eyes in the same shape as his.

My eager stare wanders back toward Morgan, the woman who Noah chose to marry for life. There's this grace about her, a woman appearing comfortable in her own skin with a bold fashion choice of all-white for a child's birthday party. Her hair is cut into a bob, short but sleek. She's a beautiful woman, and I hate the fact that I'm comparing myself to her. I'm *not* that woman. I don't fall into this trap. I know my worth, except of late, the worth has been blurred.

The jealousy, unapologetic with its presence, has been this constant burning sensation inside my chest refusing to leave. It's arrival, unannounced, stems from his text of sleeping at Olivia's. Considering there are plenty of hotels, I don't understand why he chose a sofa over a comfortable bed. Unless, of course, he was in a comfortable bed with Olivia.

And then standing only a few feet away is the woman he chose over me.

Watching Morgan furtively, my headspace becomes a negative playground, not realizing I've torn to shreds the napkin which has been sitting on the table in front of me.

Excusing myself from Rocky and his rambling about LA women and their breasts, I head into the kitchen to distract myself momentarily. After tidying up and loading up the dishwasher just to help Charlie out, I walk back outside, feeling slightly better.

I sit on the top step with a plate of food in hand, watching the kids play around the yard. They are having so much fun without a care in the world as their laughter filters through. It's such a vast difference to my life back in Paris, a real sense of family as I look on.

Beside me, I hear a ruffle, and Jessa is trying to dip a wand into a tube while trying to blow bubbles to no avail. With a frustrated pout, she appears on the verge of crying.

"If you dip it in long enough and pull it out slowly, you can blow the bubbles," I say, gently.

Her big eyes stare back at me as she does exactly that, a bubble floating in the air, much to her amusement.

"Do you know my daddy?"

"I know your daddy. He's my good friend."

"I have a best friend, but she's a girl. Her name is Ella. If a boy and a girl are best friends, they have to get married and have babies."

I didn't know how to break it to the kid. Life isn't that simple.

"Jessa, what are you doing?" Morgan stomps toward us, yanking Jessa away from me, her eyes blazing with anger.

"Mommy, I'm just talking to Daddy's best friend. They're going to get married and have babies."

Morgan's furious gaze shifts from Jessa to me. Her eyes are narrowed, rigid, and her usually pale skin is flushed. Beside her, Jessa is quiet but scowls as Morgan's grip tightens around her small arm.

"Um, no, I think you understood that all wrong, Jessa," I try to correct her with a friendly smile.

"Are you calling my child a liar?" Morgan smolders with resentment.

"Of course not," I say, trying to remain calm. "She's just exaggerated the whole married and kids' thing."

"Jessa, please go say happy birthday to Amelia. We need to go."

"But, Mommy, I want to stay with Daddy's best friend," she pouts, crossing her arms.

"Now, Jessa."

Jessa runs off while firing off some childish names to her mother.

"Listen, it wasn't—"

"So, you're fucking my ex-husband? Oh, wait a minute, we're still married, so you're fucking my husband."

"Morgan, it's not—"

"You've had your eye on him since the moment I walked into his life. How does it feel to be second best?"

My confidence is shattered, the pain rippling through

me as the woman who will forever be tied to the man I crave tells me I'm nothing. I can't let her see me broken, and so with every fiber in my being, I muster up the courage to defend myself.

"I've stayed out of Noah's life for the last three years. If your marriage fell apart, it has nothing to do with me. As for now, yes, I'm friends with Noah again. I'm not going to apologize for that."

I walk away with my head held high, escaping to the house to calm down. My nerves begin to control my movements, my trembling hands to a fast-beating heart. My emotions jump from feeling insecure to angry, and I hate that she made me feel that way.

Inside the kitchen, I scour the top cupboard for any liquor I can get my hands on. Something to take the edge of if I'm going to last another two hours surrounded by screaming children and the memory of Noah's wife telling me I'm second best.

With the bottle in my hand, a noise behind me stops me in my tracks. I turn around as Eric is standing across the room.

"We need to talk."

'Not know, Eric, please," I beg with glassed eyes. "I need a drink."

"Are you screwing my brother?"

My head lifts to meet his stern gaze, the shock drying my mouth. "Eric..."

"How long has this being going on?"

"It's not what you think."

"You've been lying to me!" he yells, hurt riddling his face. "I had to find out over dinner when my brother said he's leaving Allegra for you."

"Why... why would he say that?"

"I don't know, Kate, you tell me?"

"Eric." I clutch my stomach, unable to ignore the sharp pains. "Dominic and I are over. You don't understand. We were fooling around. It's complicated and so over."

"Over? According to him, he wants to move to Paris to be with you. That sounds far from over, don't you think?"

"Eric, I haven't spoken to Dominic since—"

"I don't understand you. You're fucking my brother, but you're trying to chase Noah? Do you even know how that looks?"

The hurt manifests throughout me from someone who's supposed to be my friend. My words are caught in my throat, my tough exterior crumbling into a piled heap around me.

"Don't you dare judge me!" I sputter with frustration. "You're just like Noah. Quick to believe everyone else but never me, right?"

"You haven't denied it?"

"You know what, Eric? Yes, I was fucking your brother. We had an agreement, and it selfishly suited my lifestyle. Was it a mistake? I don't know. But I never asked him to leave his wife. As for Noah, I never chase a man. I learned a long time ago that it only leads to heartbreak."

I walk away from Eric, wanting to head back home. If that's what I should call it, home, or a place where I can escape. But instead, I disappear into Lex's office, a place he told me was mine to use and fall into a heap of tears.

I moved my flight to Monday night, desperate to leave and get back home. Without going into too much detail with Lex, he understands and doesn't press me to stay. As for

Charlie, she was furious at Morgan and also Eric. I hate that she was dragged into this mess, but it's impossible to hide it from her since I'm staying at her place.

Early Monday morning, I drive with Lex to the office, willing my head to be buried in work. I turned off my phone last night, something I hadn't done in forever, and distracted myself with the girls for my last night here.

It was almost lunchtime, and I isolated myself in one of the smaller boardrooms with my laptop. Lex has several meetings leaving me to work alone, which is exactly what I need. The silence and the click of my fingers against the keyboard is a like a drug so desperate to ease the pain trying to kill me. Therefore, the more I type, the more control I feel like I have over my life.

The door swings open, much to my disapproval at worker's ignorance and their inability to knock. I'm about to abuse the rude person when I look up and see Noah standing at the door.

He closes the door behind him, appearing tired without having shaved. His beard is unkempt, and he's still dressed in a pair of jeans and white tee with a baseball cap on his head.

"Noah, how is Nash?" I stand, worried at his disheveled appearance, thinking the worst.

"Did you tell Morgan we're getting married?"

"What?" I shake my head in confusion. "No. It was a misunderstanding."

"Jesus fucking Christ, Kate!" he yells, his fists curled into a ball. "She called me last night, telling me everything. She's threatening to take Jessa away from me."

The hurt falls like an avalanche. I don't even know how to defend myself. I look up, and he's staring at me with resentment. I feel the heat rising to my cheeks and pray it isn't noticeable. I cough and then push my hair back behind my ear, even though it's already there.

"I never said that," I tell him, stunned by the conversation. "Jessa said those words."

"She said you said Jessa lied."

"You know what? How dare you, Noah, take her side without even listening to what I have to say."

He fails to trust me or even think I'd ever do something to jeopardize his family. I've barely been able to keep myself together the last twenty-four hours, and now I learn he can't even trust me? He'll take the word of his jealous ex-wife, or should I say, wife, over his best friend who has wanted nothing but the best for him.

"I never said those words. She's three, Noah. Did it ever occur to you that maybe she confused what I said?"

"Why were you even talking to her?"

"I have work to do. Please leave the office."

"What do you want me to do? I get several calls from Morgan accusing me of being in a romantic relationship with you. She thinks we're getting married and having a kid. Then she tells me you said Jessa is a liar."

"Believe what you want to believe. This is exactly what I was afraid of."

"She's her mother. You can't possibly understand what that's like." The second it leaves his lips, I bow my head to stop the pain from consuming me whole.

"You're right. I'll never understand what it's like to be a mother. But I understand what it's like to love someone, be honest, and treat people with respect. I've only wanted the best for you, Noah, always, and you can believe whoever you want to believe. I didn't sign up for this. In fact, I've been avoiding exactly this. Now, if you'll excuse me, I need to leave."

I close my laptop, not even shutting it down and pulling the cord out of the wall. Walking in silence, he continues to stare at me without a word.

"So, you're leaving to go back to Paris?"

I carry my laptop in my arms, staring at him with a pained gaze. "The crazy thing is, Noah, I was willing to wait for you. Just like you asked."

"And now, what?" His tone is unforgiving and fueled with animosity. "You'll run back to him?"

"I'm not going to chase heartbreak, Noah, with you or Dominic."

I never claimed to be wise with my heart, but I do recognize it breaking into a million pieces. Swallowing the lump inside my throat, I try to escape the man who has held me hostage with just his penetrating stare.

"I'd rather be on my own."

EIGHTEEN

KATE

Arriving back in Paris brings on a different wave of emotions.

A place, once so pure and beautiful in my eyes, now brings nothing but loneliness. It seems like everywhere I look, people are living their best lives. Laughter fills the streets, and couples walk hand in hand, gazing lovingly at each other with the spontaneous kisses to show their affection.

My resentment grows deeper, and patience wears thin. I no longer smile at strangers nor offer to step aside in a crowded street. Flowers bring little joy, the bunches which sit in buckets on the sidewalk seem like a ploy to get people to buy happiness. All of these things, combined, make Paris seem like the most miserable place on Earth.

My life is supposed to have been sorted by now. None of this was meant to happen. I've protected myself for as long as I could, avoiding exactly this—heartbreak.

And every part of me aches for a man, someone across an entire ocean, someone who has always been my safety net and held onto me when I'd lost my way.

The very man who used my insecurities against me, against us.

The heartache follows me wherever I go, never genuinely leaving my mind until momentarily I forget because someone else demands my attention. But then it hits me like a bolt of lightning, ferocious and unapologetic, always leading back to Noah.

In a city known as the romance capital of the world, my heart has become an open wound, but life, like always, forces me to move on.

There's no time to dwell on anything with everyone demanding my time. Once again, my absence causes additional stress, and as soon as the plane touches the tarmac, my phone hasn't stopped. Texts and emails to meetings scheduled every moment I have spare, to last-minute business trips to London and Rome over the next week. I've fallen back into the lifestyle I've known, but the loneliness will find me each night I lie wide awake, wishing this pain to disappear.

I arrive at the office at seven in the morning. Sleep barely found me last night, three hours to be exact. I woke up with no appetite but managed to eat something small and opted for intense cardio instead of my usual yoga.

"Kate," Emile calls my name as she stands at my door with a sympathetic gaze. "Permettez à votre cœur de ressentir la douleur. Alors vous saurez s'il vaut la peine de se battre."

Allow my heart to feel the pain. Then you'll know if it's worth fighting for.

The words repeat in my head, yet that's all I've thought since the moment I left the States. Every ounce of my pain is because of him. I feel like I've been fighting this uphill battle. Noah leads a complicated life, and me being with him doesn't fit the equation no matter how many times I run it through my head. Nothing adds up, and I'm not one to believe in signs, but I take this as the hazardous yellow sign staring me in the face.

I no longer want to discuss this, tired of the vicious cycle my emotions are caught up in. Misery really does love company, so I tell Emile to mark me as unavailable while I walk into the boardroom and close the door behind me. Only Charlie has called me repeatedly, but I told her the discussion is closed. There's nothing left to say, even to Eric, who I hold back from contacting since our heated fallout over Dominic.

Boredom finds me once again, this meeting a waste of time. The CFO rambles on about numbers, his voice alone putting me to sleep. His team is starting to piss me off, and it will be only a matter of time before I let this moron go. He rose in the ranks thanks to management before I stepped in. I can see through his immaturity and his narcissistic behavior. He lacks any management style, and it shows in his turnover in staff. The rambling and pathetic excuses for budget restraints last five hours. By the time they all leave the room, Lex remains on the line wanting to talk further.

"Are you prepared for London on Monday? Jerry can be quite a shark but don't let him deter you during the meeting," Lex informs me.

Great, just what I need. Another man with a small dick trying to control the world around him.

"I'm prepared." I breathe heavily, annoyed at having to deal with such arrogance. "I know his tactics, and frankly, if I don't see improvements, I'm happy to show him the door. I don't have time to waste nor fall behind on this project."

"Agreed," Lex says, then pauses. "And everything is okay with you?"

"I'm fine."

"Listen, Charlotte is worried, and you know her heart is in the right place."

"Is that her telling you to pass that on? Look..." I raise my tone only to realize who I'm talking to, "... I'm fine. If everyone will just let me be and stop worrying, I'll move just like I always do."

"Okay, I understand. It's my job to check in on you as a boss and a friend."

"I appreciate it," I assure Lex. "But I'm an adult. I'll sort out my personal life. So, don't worry about it affecting my work."

"I'm never worried, Kate. I've always trusted you to perform. But as the family member of a man who's like a brother to me, I will tell you Noah is hurting just as much."

Lex saying his name reminds me again of how intricate our ties are. It isn't just Noah and me. Too many people are invested.

"I'm sorry to hear that," I counter, only for anger to swell inside of me. "Actually, no, I'm not. For once, I did nothing wrong. He should've trusted me and given me an opportunity to defend myself, but he chooses Morgan, repeatedly. And you know what, I may never be a mother, but that choice doesn't make me less of a human being."

And I'd said all the words to the wrong man. Lex is simply the messenger, the one I've chosen to unleash my anger on. I expect him to reprimand me for yelling at him, but he simply stays quiet.

"Shit, Lex," I whisper, closing my eyes. "I'm sorry."

"It's okay, Kate."

I take a deep breath, willing to control my mood swings. I've always believed that self-control is a strength, and calmness is a mastery. It may have taken me years to have come to this revelation, yet truth be told, I wouldn't have succeeded in the business world without it.

"I should go. I'd really appreciate it if you forget all about my outburst and things go back to normal."

"Easier said than done." He chuckles softly. "You've witnessed too many of my less-finer moments, so I guess it's your turn."

"I don't think I'll ever live up to your moments. I believe you punching Julian in the face comes a close first to waking up in a bed with Victoria Preston."

"Please don't remind me," he drags over the phone. "Promise me something? You'll call Charlotte later. She's worried and stuck in the middle of you two because she loves you both. Just let her know you'll be okay. I don't like to see her upset."

"I promise," I say before ending the call.

And the truth is, I have no idea if I'll be okay. It's been four days since I left, and I'm not any closer to feeling better. All I've managed to do is ignore the stabbing pain inside and try to breathe with a punctured heart.

The walk home is uneventful, unlike the other Friday nights. People still go about their business, laughing and dancing in the streets ignoring me as I walk past with a judgmental expression because I'm heading to an empty apartment. I've barely eaten today, making my mood unpleasant and snippy, surviving on only coffee and mints. I drag my heels toward my apartment without the usual takeout in hand to lift my head and see Dominic at my door.

My limbs are frozen on the spot, restricting my breathing as it catches in my throat with every pound inside my chest. Surely, this is a figment of my imagination. I draw my eyes up from his shoes, scaling his charcoal pants, past his light blue business shirt until my gaze fixes on the deep brown eyes staring back at me. The hairs on my arms stand at attention as chills march down my spine. I can't deny his sexy appearance, but with that comes memories I'd rather forget.

"What are you doing here?"

"Kate, we need to talk."

"No, Dominic," I contest, keeping my distance. "We did talk."

"I know Allegra came to you. She told me, the question is, why didn't you?"

My anger is trumped by exhaustion. How did my life take this sudden turn, caught in some vicious love triangle with no exit in sight? All I want is a Friday night alone to watch some violent movie and pretend I'm back to my old self again.

I clutch my purse tightly, trying to rein in my frustration. "Your wife ambushed me in my office. Then she gives me her blessing to fuck you but for the two of you to stay married. I don't know what part of that I should answer?"

Dominic moves swiftly toward me, closing the gap between us. Letting out a breath, I'm trying to ignore everything about him I once craved, the power he holds around us because no matter how I spin the scenario in my head, he'll never be what my heart so desperately craves.

"I can't stop thinking about you," he admits with a thirsty stare. "Every. Fucking. Day. Just think about what Allegra said. We can still have this great life together, you and me. The way you've always wanted."

I raise my hand to stop him, my body bursting with fury. "The way I've always wanted? Four years ago, I'd have done anything for you to want me. But you've conditioned me to want only one thing from you."

"And do you still want that?" He inches closer, dragging his finger across the bottom of my lip.

Our bad romance has been nothing but cheap emotions, which led to our bond being built by greed. A toxic lover, which is what Dominic is, becomes an addiction. He knows exactly how to keep me in his court begging for more each time we're together. He's learned to feed my weakness and nurture it into a vicious weed strangling my self-worth.

And despite our affair being kept a secret, it has caused more damage to the people we love, including one of my best friends—Eric. The game always needs to come to an end. There will be no winners because the rules we set up were destined for failure.

I let out a breath, tilting my head away from his touch. Taking a step back, I look at him with an unrelenting stare.

"I want to be loved entirely, for everything I am. I want to spend my life with a man and be the only woman to consume him whole. I want to make memories, feel loved, and express my love in return. I don't deserve less than that, and what you're doing is trying to make me believe that I do."

The words have finally escaped me, released from a vault buried in the dark pits of my soul. For all these years, I've refuted love only to realize I can't live without it.

A sound startles both of us, my head shifts to the entrance where Noah is standing with his duffle bag on the ground. Wide-open eyes reflect everything he feels, and I know instantly that his mind drifts to a jealous place in which the sight of Dominic and me has sliced him open like a sharp knife.

His posture stiffens, fists clenched toward his sides, drunk in anger as his eyes blaze a torch, and it's only a matter of time before his fury unleashes.

Dominic's expression shifts, almost as if I can see the wheels turning in Noah's head.

"Let me guess?" Dominic shakes his head in disbelief. "So, is he the reason why?"

"You need to leave."

"I'm not leaving, we're not over," he orders in a decidedly odd tone

"You fucking heard her." Noah moves closer toward us, prompting Dominic to back off. My pulse begins to race from nerves as I purposely stand between them, knowing all too well a fight could break out at any moment.

"Who the fuck are you to tell me to leave?"

"Because I'm the man who respects Kate for who she is and what she wants. I'm not the one proposing she fuck me while I stay married to keep up appearances."

Dominic's anger ripples through his clenched fists before I see him swing at Noah. Noah ducks his head just in time, connecting his fist with Dominic's jaw. Blood ripples out until I shout at them both to stop, my hands pushing Dominic away and trying to create distance from Noah.

"Go, now," I warn Dominic, examining his face quickly. "Please, just go back to your wife. That's where you belong. Not with me."

Like an animal calling defeat, his nostrils flare violently as he takes one step away from us. "You've always come back to me, Kate. It won't take long for you to remember why."

I release the breath I've been holding in to watch him disappear down the stairwell and out of the building. My head falls, unable to look Noah in the eye because there are so many things that need to be said.

He broke me first.

I'm still *angry*.

And most of all—I hate that I miss him.

Reaching into my purse, I retrieve my key and unlock the door. I motion for Noah to come inside, keeping my words at bay. I quickly head for the freezer as he follows me and grab a tub of ice-cream since it's all I have, placing it in his hand.

"Did you call him?"

"No," I answer, defeated. "I didn't."

"So, he just came here? Just showed up at your door."

I nod, keeping silent.

"I need to know what happened?"

"Nothing happened. Absolutely nothing at all."

Noah retracts his hand, wincing in pain. His jealous streak is exhausting. Lowering my head, I feel an emotional wave of tears but hold back because I'm *not* that woman. I don't cry over men, especially in front of them.

"You're telling me that the two of you stood in silence and said nothing? That he didn't remind you how great it is to fuck him? That what you have is amazing. He's the love of your life. He can give you things I possibly can't?"

The tear finally escapes gracefully down my cheek and onto my lips. I can't hold it back. I could blame the exhaustion, the lack of sleep, but deep down inside, I know it's because I'm standing beside a man who I can't live without.

It hurts to breathe without him.

This much I finally know.

"You want to know what I said?" I search Noah's eyes, begging for a sign that everything I feel means something, that it's not something superficial. It's not lust, and it's more than just friendship. "I told him that I deserved more. I wanted more. I want to feel the love of a man whose heart only beats for me. I want a life, memories. I want it all. And the worst part of it is, all I could think about is you. The same person who makes me feel less than what I am when you fail to listen to me and tell me I can't possibly understand what it's like to be a mother."

"What I said..." he utters, dropping his shoulders and ducking his chin, "... was uncalled for. I'm so angry at myself for fearing the worst, for losing control, and for taking it out on the one person who has always believed in me. I've allowed other people to control my own emotions before I even have a chance. And all it's done is push you away. Fuck, Kate. I hate myself for doing this to you."

I can't look into his eyes, terrified that if I do, he'll break me again. But this isn't all about me. Slowly, I lift my head to stare at a man who has openly admitted his weakness, embraced his vulnerability to show me how much he doesn't want to lose what we have. I realize now, despite his callous words bringing me down, the burden he carries is far greater. He was, and still is, fighting to be the best man he can be for his kids. His greatest fear of being an absent father has driven him to the depths of despair.

Expressing his pain and showing his courage to turn up here in Paris is far from comfortable. He's taken a risk, even though we left things the way we did, and I love him even more for fighting for what he wants and never giving up.

Even if I have to finally admit he's fighting for *me*.

"I know you feel something, Noah. I no longer deny that... I'm just..."

"What, Kate?" he urges, drawing closer to me. "If we're going to do this, you and me, we need to be completely honest with each other."

Noah is right. We can't play these games anymore. There's too much on the line. My heart is hanging by a thread, just one snap, and it's completely broken.

"The way you make me feel," I whisper, holding my

breath. "I'm losing who I thought I wanted to be. It's like when I'm with you, nothing else matters."

Noah caresses my cheek, wiping away the one tear I allowed to escape. The touch is warm, a blanket keeping me safe and comforted. How can I tell him it's all or nothing? How can I admit to my best friend that there's only one road we can travel down, and I want to be beside him now and forever?

"I love who I am when I'm around you," he expresses as his lips curve upward. "You bring out the best in me."

I stare into his eyes, allowing myself to lose myself in him. As he leans forward, my pulse races, craving him so much. His lips graze against mine, soft and teasingly. He withdraws but stays a breath away, leaving the spot he kissed burning like the touch of a flame. It pulsates through me, spreading like wildfire as his stare deepens, and my heart belongs only to him.

"If we do this..."

"If we do this," he repeats in a small breath.

"It's all in," I tell him, throwing my heart into the battle-field with everything to lose. "Too much is at stake, and too many people will be involved in our lives for us to fall apart without hurting those around us."

He bows his head, and when he raises his eyes to meet mine again, a glaze shimmers around his pupils.

"We've both watched each other live our lives with other people. I watched you walk away, move to Paris, fall into the arms of another man who doesn't deserve you."

"And I've watched you fall in love with another woman, marry, and have her child. I may not have been around when it fell apart, or when you ran into somebody else's arms, and to be honest, I'm glad I wasn't around for that."

"Our life will be complicated. Kids, ex-wives, ex-lovers, friends... are you sure you can handle my baggage?"

I run my hands through his hair like I've done a dozen times before, but this time it feels so different. Wrapping my hands around his neck, he rests his hands on my hips. "Noah Mason, you're worth it."

His lips brush against mine again, and softly, he kisses me, a kiss which melts away any doubt I have left in us. A kiss which seals our fate and makes us one.

"So," I breathe, still holding onto him. "What now?"

"What? One kiss and you're bored of me already?" he teases, kissing me again before pulling away.

I laugh, grazing his bottom lip with my finger. "One thing I can admit is that I'm never bored with you. I'm in Paris, and you're in LA."

He releases a sigh, knowing our battle to be together is far from over.

"I'm here now."

"Yes, you are, but for how long?"

"I have a flight out tomorrow at four, but for tonight, I want to take you out on a real date."

"A real date?" I grin with an appraising glance. "How romantic of you. Do I get a clue?"

He shakes his head. "Not one single clue. I'll be back in an hour. Be dressed and ready."

"Wait, what kind of dressed?" I ask, still holding onto him. "You know, my wardrobe ranges from Dior to a potato sack."

"You have a potato sack in your closet?"

"Yes, it's called a failed purchase when Eric told me muumuus were in."

Cupping my face with his hands, he kisses me deeply before pulling away, leaving me aching for more. "I'm sure you look sexy in a potato sack. But perhaps, to ease your mind, something more formal."

"But why do you have to go?" I beg, clutching his shirt with my hands. "I like you here."

"I have something to take care of. And if I don't go, you'll end up on all fours complaining about why you can't walk. We've got plenty of time for that to happen, but only one night in Paris."

With a final kiss, he exits my apartment, leaving me in my kitchen as I touch my lips, reminiscing about our kiss.

A night in Paris with Noah Mason is just what my heart so desperately aches for. My two greatest loves, together for one night, and with that thought, bringing the happiness I finally deserve, I realize it's all too late.

I've fallen in love with my best friend.

And there's no turning back.

NINETEEN

KATE

"Have I told you how beautiful you look tonight?"

On a beautiful Parisian night, Noah kisses my hand as we stroll along the street to an unknown destination. At least, unbeknownst to me. Noah knows exactly where we're going.

In the eyes of someone so blissfully happy with a gorgeous man beside her, Paris has transformed into the most romantic city. As we walk past other couples, we nod, almost like a secret society of couples. Everything surrounding us feels so different. The streetlights are like stars above us, the flowers in the gardens are in full bloom, and perhaps, somewhere floating around us is cupid with his bow and arrow.

I'm drunk on happiness and not even sorry.

"We're here."

I follow Noah inside the building, past the concierge who graciously escorts us on the elevator ride up. As we reach the top floor, he holds the door open as Noah requests I close my eyes. Guiding me through a doorway, he tells me to open my eyes moments later.

We're standing on a terrace surrounded by greenery and twinkling lights scattered around them. In the middle of the space is a small round table adorned with a white tablecloth and lit with candles. A bottle of champagne is sitting in a chilled bucket next to the plates and silver cutlery.

It's all so breathtaking until my eyes glance sideways to sweeping views of the Eiffel Tower. Perfect and oh so romantic.

"You know, I've never been wooed before." I sigh dreamily as Noah pushes the chair out for me to take a seat.

"Not even in the 1950s when that saying was used last?"

"Such a charming date," I counter hopelessly. "I'm certain that part of wooing isn't roasting the said subject."

"Okay, I'm sorry." He pouts, touching my hand while my stomach flutters in excitement. "You're stunning, and I want all your clothes off by midnight."

I chuckle, dropping my head foolishly. "More like it. Tell me, how did you make this all happen?"

"Pulled some strings. I know a few important people."

"I'm impressed." My smile wavers while my head does the math of how long we have together. "So, you're only here for one night?"

Noah places both his hands on mine, easing the nerves of what we're doing. "We have a long road ahead of us. Let's enjoy the journey. Someone once told me to be present, in the moment."

With a knowing grin, he pops open the champagne and pours some into my flute, then into his own. As the champagne graces my lips, even the taste is different. For once, it's purpose is to celebrate rather than drown out my sorrows over a failed love life.

A waiter serves us a meal, placing it in front of us. The aromas of traditional French cuisine engulf my senses as Noah encourages me to eat. My first bite is like heaven, and given my lack of appetite earlier on, I'm absolutely starving right now.

"Tell me about work, Haden, and Presley. I read an article saying that e-Books are profiting and publishers are inundated."

"Books will always be in demand. It's going well. No surprises, the romance sector is very profitable."

"Wait a minute..." I place my fork down. "Does Noah Mason read romance?"

He purses his lips behind a smirk. "I've read maybe one or two. Just to understand the market."

"You're quite the perfect man right now. Minus the ex-wife and all," I tease, picking up my fork to finish my meal. "I haven't spoken to Presley for a while without Haden in the room annoying her." I answer his question, then continue with, "So, everything's going well then with work?"

"Hmm, it's okay."

I hear the hesitation in his voice. "But? You can talk to me."

"There's something in the pipeline. I don't want to speak too prematurely until it's finalized."

I understand his hesitation. The business world is cutthroat. One minute you're about to make the best deal of your life, and the next, it's pulled out from underneath you.

"And what about you?" He changes the subject. "How did it go with Mr. Auvray?"

"We're making headway. A few improvements to try and draw some attention to the winery."

"It's beautiful and an easy sell. People are looking for

experiences, the type they can splash all over their social media and brag about. This is the market you want."

"You're the expert in that area, so I wholeheartedly agree. I know when we stayed there, I've never experienced such exquisite food. Did Lex tell you he offered the chef his own chain of restaurants?"

"He certainly did." Noah chuckles. "That man is unstoppable."

"Yeah, some cousin-in-law you have."

"Some boss you have."

We both laugh at the same time, any tension I have built up in my mind easing as the night goes on. We've been the best of friends, and that's what makes this all the easier. He knows me inside and out, just as I know him.

"How are things with Olivia and baby Nash?"

"He's doing well. Eating like a machine, or shall I say drinking like a machine. Olivia is okay, I guess."

"What do you mean she's okay? Have you asked her how she's doing?"

"Yes, she has a lot on her mind. They want her back at work, but her job is in the air, meaning long hours."

"Noah, she's all alone trying to raise a baby for the first time. I can only imagine how difficult that must be. I remember when Presley had her baby, and she and Haden weren't a couple yet, she struggled, especially when she went back to work. Olivia needs all the support she can get. What's that saying? It takes a village to raise a family or something like that."

His eyes linger, the soft hazel mesmerizing as he falls deep into thought. "So, you really don't want kids of your own?"

I'm taken aback by the topic of kids being raised, specifically about me. I've always been honest with my opinions on this matter, and nothing has changed that. Noah has his hands full with two young kids, a career, and now a girl-friend in Paris.

"Are you telling me this is a deal-breaker?"

"No, I'm just asking, to be clear."

"To be honest, it's never something I've strived for. I love children, but I never viewed family as something you have to physically give birth to. My father was adopted as was one of my brothers. The love of a family does not have to be defined by the pressure of society. We can equally love no matter who we choose to welcome to our family."

"But if it happened, by accident?"

I laugh, wanting to strangle him. I can almost see my annoying best friend emerging with his ridiculous questions. "Find a different hole, buddy. I guess I'd have the child. I don't know how to answer that."

"Back to the *hole* thing..."

"Such an optimist, Mr. Mason."

Our dessert is served, but Noah suggests we take it to the lounge chairs along with our champagne. As we sit with the stunning view of the Paris skyline in front of us, Noah places his arm around me and draws me closer. Planting a soft kiss on the top of my head, I bury my face into his chest, living for the moment of feeling safe in his arms, untouch-able by the world surrounding us.

"I don't want to leave," he whispers, a strain in his voice. "But I have to."

I raise my head, staring into his eyes. "We'll make it work, I promise. But you've got to be patient. We both have such hectic lives. We're never going to be like everyone else, so that comparison needs to stop right here. We have to make the best of our situation."

His lips find mine, a kiss filled with a fiery passion.

When he pulls away, I attempt to catch my breath as his mouth wanders to my neck, kissing my skin with urgency.

"Noah, we can't here."

"Why not?"

"Because of people."

"There are no people."

I look behind us. The place is vacant. The waiters have disappeared.

"But there were people?"

"They won't be back," he murmurs, still buried in my neck.

Noah retracts, his eyes wild and untamed. "I promise you. They won't be back. I paid them not to be back."

His fingers graze against my shoulder, pulling the strap of my dress down. He watches it fall past my shoulders, the bite of his lip holding my gaze. "I've been waiting for what feels like a lifetime for this moment. Once we..."

"We can never go back," I finish for him.

I know exactly how he feels.

We're finally in sync.

His kisses trail my skin, igniting every sense. My hands wrap around his head as I moan softly. We lay beside each other, lost in a sea of kisses. I never imagined how passionate foreplay could be by the simple act of kissing. It's all so juvenile, and I love every second of it. There's no rush, no pressure, just two people learning how to become one.

Noah's hand slides down my arm, past the curve of my breast, and rests on my thigh. I wiggle beneath him until he's lying on top with a penetrating gaze. No words need to be said, the silence speaking volumes as my hands wander toward the button of his pants. Noah groans in my mouth while he reaches below and slides my dress over my thighs.

My heart is beating like a loud drum, the anticipation

too much for my aching body to handle. Our eyes can't break the stare until he brushes against my entrance and enters me whole. My back arches, a delicious moan escaping me as his lips find their way back to the crook of my neck. I wither under his touch, the intensity of such an intimate moment is all so new to me.

We move in sync, our bodies crumble into this perfect mold of who we have become. And with a penetrating stare, I beg of him, "Together."

We both finish as if our whole being depends on it. The ripples of delight spread through every inch of my body, the euphoria being a constant state of high I never want to come down from.

Noah falls softly on top of me, and all I can hear is the sound of his beating heart.

A sound so pure like a melody I've known all my life.

"Noah," I whisper. "That was perfect."

He brushes a loose strand of hair away from my face.

"I wanted our first time to be perfect," he says softly, then follows with a devious smirk. "But, since that's now over, it's time to get dirty. Are you ready to head home? I've got plans for you, and sleep isn't one of them."

I laugh beneath him. "Show me what you got, cowboy."

TWENTY

KATE

My breath hitches as my head falls to the pillow in pure bliss.

I can barely open my eyes, every muscle sore with a delicious ache from a man who has ravaged me nonstop since the moment we stepped foot in my apartment.

"You've killed me." My throat is dry, desperate for water, though I can't move a single limb. "Am I even alive?"

Noah snickers beside me, running his finger along the side of my breast, causing me to shiver in delight. My eyes are still closed as his lips circle around my nipples, a moan escaping me once again.

"I hate to burst your bubble, but Necrophilia isn't my thing," he informs me.

My phone buzzes on the nightstand. Reaching over to the side, I bring it close to me and open one eye to see the number on the screen, sending it straight to voicemail.

"You're a wanted woman. Your screen is covered in text and email notifications."

"I know, it's like they don't know I'm having the most

intense orgasm ever," I say with resentment. "Selfish bastards."

I manage to twist on my side, bringing my face toward his chest to feel his skin. He smells so masculine, and despite my earlier complaint of being ravaged, a stir between my legs sends mixed signals. This is insane.

"I wish you didn't have to leave."

"I wish I didn't have to either. But I have work and Jessa," he mentions while stroking my hair with his fingertips. "Plus, I'm thinking of flying to San Francisco to see Nash next weekend."

"Have you asked Olivia to move closer to you?"

He continues to play with my hair, letting out a sigh. "I don't know how to bring it up. Olivia is a reasonable woman, nothing at all like Morgan. I guess I've been preoccupied with a certain somebody who's lying naked beside me."

My lips part into a loving smile, then slowly, I kiss his chest wishing things were different.

"Far from me to intrude, but what if you can compromise? If she can move closer, you can help, as can your mom. Some of the smaller carriers only fly on the West Coast. One of our business associates owns a charter company specializing in corporate traveling. Perhaps, a company like that would mean that she could still work but be home each night."

Noah stares at me avidly, pressing his lips together.

"I'm sorry... it's your life and—"

"Hey..." he interrupts, lifting my chin, so our eyes meet. "Don't be sorry. I love your intelligence, your ability to see a situation and find solutions. You've always been this headstrong woman, but with the biggest goddamn heart I know. It's why I love you."

I fall silent at his words. It isn't the first time I've heard the comments leave his mouth but in a different context. He's said it as a best friend when there was no romantic interest in me whatsoever. But now, those three words sound entirely different.

"I love you, Kate, and before you say anything in which you don't have to say anything, I want you to know that this isn't new to me. I've known this fact for a long time, but life panned out differently. So many times throughout my marriage, I wanted to reach out to you, but I couldn't. So instead, I stalked you online."

"Noah—"

"Let me finish, please. Morgan and I never truly fit. We weren't easy together, but I gave our relationship the benefit of the doubt and because others told me marriage wasn't easy. You have to work hard for it. But I knew deep down inside that both of us were working too hard to save something we never truly had." He takes a deep breath, then continues, "She was right last week when she called me about the party. She said she never had a chance because it was always you. And there were countless nights when I'd lay there and think about you, about us and what we had. The guilt ate away at me because I felt like I wasn't giving Morgan a chance because you were on my mind. So, just so you know... this has been a long time coming for me."

All along, I was jealous of a woman who won Noah's heart. And last week, when she called me second best, her own insecurities were being projected. The saying stays true, you don't know what battle someone is fighting behind the scenes.

"But this is new to me," I confess, swallowing the lump in my throat. "For the longest of time, I've buried the memories of us and refused for them to surface. I purposely distanced myself not to see your new life. I built my life to focus on only me because the thought of having my heart broken again was just not going to happen. It's why I agreed to the arrangement with Dominic. But you did break me, Noah. It's hard to know that you were falling in love with someone else. And now..."

"And now?"

"I'm scared. I don't want to lose my best friend, but..." I whisper with bated breath. "I love you."

Noah crashes his lips on mine, leaving me to gasp. My hands feverishly run through his hair while ignoring my weak limbs as I climb on top and ride him once again. In the throes of passion, we can't get enough. Our bodies move in sync. My bedsheets are strewn across the floor while he fucks me sideways, on all fours, carrying me to the window as he devours my body against the glass.

I've fallen to my knees, taking him all in. Licking every inch of him before we wind up in the shower, and it becomes my turn to be worshipped.

And once we exhaust our physical self, we lay in bed talking all night.

"Do you remember when I flew to Manhattan?" Noah murmurs with his hands in my hair as my head rests on his chest, listening to the sound of his beating heart. "The time you had an emotional breakdown over someone who shall remain nameless?"

"Uh... don't remind me."

"I knew then I felt more. Everything with you was always easy. But it's like there was this line between us, and I kept telling myself I only wanted to cross it because I'm not supposed to. The forbidden line which would've changed everything between us."

"I wouldn't have let you, anyway." I sigh, watching my

fingers caress his perfectly sculpted chest. "You were confused. And I loved what we had, this unbreakable friendship, or at least, that's what I thought at the time. I've never had anyone like you in my life. Eric doesn't count."

"I heard, from Charlie, about your altercation. Have you spoken to him since?"

I shake my head, keeping quiet for a moment. "The thing is, Eric was right. I hid my affair with Dominic because I was ashamed and had everything to lose. And it was never a competition between you and him. I never felt safe with Dominic, he was just there as someone to help me forget."

Beneath me, Noah's body stiffens. It's a sore subject to discuss, especially now that I know how Noah feels about me. My fingers glide across his chest, tracing his skin with a touch rather than words. Moments later, I feel him relax, his chest rising and falling at his usual pace.

"I loathe the man," he lowers his voice.

"I know. It's over now, Noah. It's just you and me."

His lips find my forehead, a gentle kiss washing away this momentary tension.

"The night I saw you in Versailles, you have no idea how much I needed to see you."

"I had no clue about what you were going through," I say openly. "But I could see it broke you."

"It did. Can I ask you something?"

"Hmm, anything, Noah."

"Have you..." he clears his throat, his body tensing again. "Have you fucked him since that night?"

I shake my head instantly, reassuring him and not hesitating like he always claimed I had done. "I didn't, I couldn't. Everything always led back to you no matter how hard I tried to fight it. I had no idea what it meant, but it all makes sense now."

The breath he's been holding in releases. Noah has always had a jealous streak. Typical male, of course. In many ways, he reminds me of a younger Lex when Charlie was engaged to Julian.

"The night at the ball, you were so drunk. Do you remember asking me to fuck you?" he teases, a small chuckle escaping him.

"What? I asked that?" I question, surprised. "I asked you to fuck me?"

"I believe your exact words were, 'Noah, you've always wanted to fuck me. Let's do it, tonight, here."

"I wanted to fuck you at the actual ball?" Laughter escapes my lips. "I don't remember that at all."

"I could have, you had your hands all over me, but it wouldn't have been right. It would've been a Band-Aid on what we were both trying to navigate through at the time. I wanted it to be right... like tonight."

Raising my eyes to meet his, I stare into his beautiful face. "C'était la première fois parfait."

His hazel eyes flicker, the way they always do when locked in with my own.

"It was a perfect first time. And it has to be. It's you," he whispers. "You can wait a whole lifetime to feel the touch of the woman you love but every minute is worth the wait the second she's finally yours."

I release the breath I've been holding in, letting his emotions wash over me like a warm summer's breeze. "Someone should write a book about us."

"They should. I'd be the perfect book boyfriend."

A small laugh follows. "You know what a book boyfriend is?"

"Unfortunately, yes."

Our laughs echo in the room as Noah quotes romantic lines from books he has read. All the more surprising me on how knowledgeable he is in that area.

It's the perfect first date I could've asked for, but it has to come to an end like everything in life.

My eyes spring open after falling asleep sometime after dawn. I turn to see my phone, noting it's almost midday. *Shit.*

I scramble up, my head spinning as I clutch my forehead, willing it to stop. Noah exits the bathroom, dressed in a pair of jeans and a buttoned shirt. I pull the sheet toward my chest, covering my breasts and wishing he didn't have to leave. He may be in the room, but I ache for him, missing his touch. The way his lips create a frenzy within me. The way my heart beats erratically when his eyes fall upon me. We have no plan, nothing to promise our next reunion. The thought leaves me helpless, a part of me I can no longer control because now I have to factor in someone else. And not just someone else, a man who has other commitments that will always be more important than me—his children.

"I liked it better when you were naked," I tell him, watching him tie his shoes, trying to clear my mind from negative thoughts.

"Hmm, I know, but wouldn't that be awkward on the plane?"

"For you, maybe, but not for the women scoping out your junk."

"Did you just say junk?"

"Enormous penis," I pronounce clearly. "Is that more articulate for you?"

Noah shakes his head, a grin playing on his beautiful lips. "You're crazy."

"Are you sure I can't take you to the airport?"

Noah sits on the edge of the bed. "If you do, I'll never leave."

I bow my head, this crappy emotion making me want to cry or something. My stomach is twisted in knots, my fingers aimlessly turning the sheets to distract where this is going.

"Hey, listen to me." Noah cups my chin, raising my eyes to meet his. "I love you. We'll fly to see each other when we can. Please just believe in me. That's all I ask."

I kiss his lips gently, enjoying this moment because it may be our last for a while. It isn't fair to project my own selfish emotions onto him. I know he's torn, so I choose to smile to reassure him we'll be okay.

"I believe in us, okay? I love you. Now go home and FaceTime me when you get back."

Taking one more look at me, he leans in as our lips meet again before he rests his forehead on mine and takes a breath. Planting a kiss on my forehead, he finally pulls back to leave the room and my apartment.

I fall back into bed, clutching the sheets as if my life depends on it. Everything has changed, my entire world has flipped upside down. As I stare at the ceiling like I've done a million times before, I eventually fall back to sleep dreaming about Noah.

The man who has finally won my heart—completely.

TWENTY-ONE

KATE

I spent the remainder of the weekend trying to do anything to keep my hands busy and mind off the fact that Paris feels like the loneliest city in the world.

I've cleaned my entire apartment, gone shopping and to a library, drank a bottle of wine and ate a whole box of pastries, none of which left me satisfied.

With an early flight booked to London on Monday morning, I pack my suitcase and prepare my presentation. It will be good to go back home, if only for three days. I plan to catch up with my parents for dinner with the limited spare time I have.

Noah FaceTimed me when he got back home. Jessa was staying at his place for the night, so she sat beside him when we chatted, interrupting to show me this weird doll with googly eyes. Seeing the two of them together, the resemblance is uncanny. He looks happy, his eyes bright when we speak. Due to the time difference, we ended our call, and I promised to call him when I get back from London.

I've done what I have trained myself to do for the longest of times, bury my head in work to try and forget about the distance between Noah and myself. The trip to London went by quickly, a catch-up with my parents the highlight of my journey. I chose to keep my private life exactly that—private. My mother is an opinionated woman, and I came close to spilling the beans when she mentioned an old neighbor of ours is now single. The same guy I'd lost my virginity to many moons ago.

Milan was uneventful, all work and no play. The days became a hazy blur, passing by quickly until night fell. Noah called or texted me every day, but we were never in sync with his schedule as busy as mine.

Three weeks pass before we manage to be in our beds at the same time.

It's after midnight for me and dinner time for him. He's child-free, and thank God because the video call is what we both need.

"I miss you," I tell him, trying to control my breathing from a very intense self-induced orgasm.

"You have no idea," he responds, laying perfectly naked in his bed. "Just give it time."

I want to be honest, ask exactly how time would change things between us. The hard, cold reality is that I'm in Paris, and he's in LA. Time won't change that.

"Okay," I mumble as a yawn escapes me. "I'll call you tomorrow."

We hang up the phone as I fall asleep to the sound of sirens outside on the street.

Weekends are always the hardest. There's only so much I can do to occupy myself. I attend every social event just to get out of the apartment, but the craving to be in Noah's arms never leaves me.

Upon returning one night, tipsy from a gallery exhibit

that handed out free champagne, I decide I need perspective.

"Hey, Charlie."

"Uh-oh... you sound awful. Are you sick, wait... you're pregnant!"

"No, I've had a few drinks," I assure her, a slight hiccup escaping me. "Charlie, how am I going to do this?"

Over the last few weeks, I've kept mine and Noah's relationship on the down-low. It's all still new, and I want to make sure I know how I feel before involving others. But tonight, I shed light on the whole situation leaving out the part about any lovemaking since Charlie is Noah's cousin.

"Kate, you're the strongest, most loving woman I know. I know that one day when you fall in love with a man, your heart will be all his," she tells me with a smile evident in her voice. "Dominic was an infatuation, that bad habit hard to break, but he wasn't the one to love you the way you deserve. You love Noah, and his children are his world. I believe in you, and I believe you'll make a fantastic stepmother. I've seen you with my girls, and they adore you."

"But I'm here, Charlie. Am I supposed to give up my whole life for a man?"

"You'll do what your heart feels is right. When Lex and I first got back together, I also thought the same. He was in London, and I in Manhattan. And look at us now? We're in LA. Wherever the two of you are, it doesn't matter. Love always prevails."

Love always prevails.

What do I know about love? I'm an amateur.

Yes, I've said the words, but the fact that I am not running into his arms and giving up my world, does that count for anything?

"He's going stir crazy, just so you know."

"He is?" Selfish of me to feel this way, but this news somehow makes me feel better.

"Are you kidding me? The guy is crazy in love with you. You try to talk to him, and he's spaced out. He even came over the other day and agreed to watch *Romeo and Juliet* with Amelia and me."

"The one with Leonardo DiCaprio?"

"Uh-huh."

"Oh." I sigh, followed by a laugh. "How tragic."

"So, as I was saying, don't think you're alone in feeling this way."

We speak about his kids, work, and life during our calls but never really delve into our relationship since neither of us has answers.

"It'll work out, I promise," Charlie reminds me. "You'll just have that moment when it all falls into place."

I spent a few days working from Mr. Auvray's chateau. Being in Champagne brought back the nostalgia of not long ago when Noah and I spent the night chatting under the stars. Everything reminds me of him—the rustle of the trees as we walked beside them, the taste of the champagne we drank so eagerly together.

I miss him terribly, and it's true, distance does make the heart grow fonder.

A team from our company joins me, going through the changes and capital improvements on the actual property. We eat delicious food, drink copious amounts of champagne, and tell stories while soaking up the picturesque countryside.

There's little spare time to do anything on our own, but

I manage to get away for a few hours, borrowing one of the Chateau's bicycles and ride along the pebbled path admiring the scenery. I snap photographs, sending them to Noah until I brake suddenly, distracted by a chateau not too far from the Auvray's.

I take a deep breath, admiring its beauty. It has period features, detailed in stone and surrounded by a peaceful-looking garden. The lawns are manicured to perfection, the flowers blossoming, and trees are planted to provide a bit of privacy.

It looks like a picture out of a fairy tale book, housing a damsel in distress waiting for her prince to save her.

I take a selfie, something I rarely do, and post it on Instagram along with the caption I read in a magazine. 'Any home can be a castle when the King and Queen are in love.'

How perfect would it be if Noah were here? France will always own a piece of me, but without the man I love, the magic disappears. The pang hits me again, but this time it lingers for much longer.

By Monday morning, my outlook has turned bleak. We officially hit the four-week mark of being apart, and without any significant holidays plus both our workloads being busy, there isn't even a chance for a quick getaway.

I sit at my desk, typing an email when there's a knock on my door—Lex poking his head in. With an incredulous stare, my mouth falls open, surprised to see him.

"Lex? I had no idea you were coming." He steps inside, taking a seat in the chair in front of me. "Charlie didn't mention anything of the sort."

"I'm here for business."

"Sure, I can clear my schedule?"

"Please."

I look up at him, noting his serious expression. Picking

up the phone, I call Emile and ask her to clear my schedule for the rest of the day.

"Is everything okay?" she whispers before continuing, "*Lex est un homme magnifique.*"

I chuckle softly. "Off-limits, Emile."

Placing the receiver down, Lex tilts his head to the side with curiosity.

"A certain assistant of mine thinks you're beautiful," I tease with a small laugh escaping. "Where's Charlie to set her straight when you need her?"

Lex purses his lips, hiding his smile. "I'm here because I want to make you a job offer."

"I have a job," I remind him. "You know, holding down the fort in Europe. Bringing the money in."

"Let me rephrase that question... I have a proposition for you." He clears his throat, forcing me to take him seriously. "As you know, I've been wanting to expand into the hospitality industry and have my eye on acquiring some hotel chains. Now, granted, I'm looking at places we can completely overhaul and modernize with what the travel industry desperately craves."

"It makes sense. Tourism is a sure money-maker if done right."

"I want you to manage it from the ground up."

"The project?"

"No, the business. You'll be the President of the DeLuxe Group. We'll begin with acquiring their portfolio of hotels. Invest in the ones we see potential in, sell off the small chains of no interest or growth."

"That's a change... and a challenge."

I think about Noah and all the changes in my life. I'm just not sure if I want to invest my time in a new position. It's almost like starting over again.

"Since when have you ever backed down from a challenge?"

"I believe you've never allowed me permission to," I tell him with a knowing smile. "So, what's your timeline, and where do you need me?"

"I'd like handover handled here. Javier has proven himself, and if you are to say yes, I'll be speaking with him next. As for where.... the main headquarters are Los Angeles."

"Los Angeles?"

Lex waits for a response, raising his brow. "Is moving to LA a problem for you?"

"No... but..." I trail off. "You know then."

"Look, Kate. This idea didn't happen overnight. It's been two years in the making, and only a few months ago, our lawyers gave me the green light. My reason for pushing it aside is because I never had anyone worthy to run it. You know you're one of the only people I trust. You've been there with me throughout it all, and did a certain union push me to make the final decision, yes?"

"But what if I say no?"

"Then you'd be giving up on what you and Noah have. Trust me, I've done it, and it's a mistake which you'll have to live with forever. So, are you ready to call Javier in?"

Lex never takes no for an answer, and I've never let him down. The thought of moving back to the States comes with mixed trepidation. I need time to think about this.

"Can I have time to think about it?"

"I'm leaving tomorrow evening, so until midday," he informs me, standing up to leave the room. "You're born for this role. And you'll be working with an amazing team. I envision global domination. We'll start with the States, but our future will be Europe and Asia."

Lex exits my office, leaving me with a heavy weight on my shoulders.

That night, I lay in bed, unable to shut down. My mind has become a circus of cluttered thoughts, all of which lead to Noah. If I move to LA, would I live with Noah or keep our lives separate? If we do live together, does that make me a stepmother? What role will I play in his kids' lives?

And most importantly—how will I find the time to juggle what seems like a demanding job and a boyfriend too. Noah isn't exactly swimming in time, constantly trying to balance his life. If I'm with him full-time, will he have time for me, or will we fall apart from the pressure?

My thoughts become too much, and several times I want to reach out and call him to talk it through but decide against it. He's more than my best friend now—I can't unload on him like I would've before.

Eventually, I fall asleep to be awoken hours later by the morning sunrise. Once again, I avoid yoga because coffee seems more important. At the café beside my building, I order my coffee to notice a couple beside me. They are practically making out, smiling as they can't keep their hands off each other. The man turns to look at me, a polite smile in which I offer one in return. When he shifts his attention back onto his significant other, he cups her chin as Noah has done so many times to mine, and murmurs, "*J'aime qui je suis quand je suis avec toi.*"

Standing beside them, it all becomes clear. As the man tells the women in French, 'I love who I am when I'm with you,' my memories of Noah saying the same thing to me cements my decision.

I race back home, dialing his number, praying he hasn't gone to bed yet.

"Hey, you."

Noah clears this throat. "Hey, I was just thinking about you."

"I didn't wake you, did I?" My head can't even compute the time zone difference right now.

"I can't sleep," he simply says.

"I'm sorry... it's just that... I want to discuss something important."

"Go ahead."

I take a deep breath. It's now or never. "Lex offered me a position in LA. I'd be President of DeLuxe Group, and it's going to be a challenge, but—"

"Wait, you're moving to LA?"

"I'm thinking about it..."

"You're thinking about it? What's there to think about?"

"I just didn't want to push you. You have so much going on, and do you really want me knocking on your door every five minutes?"

"How many times do I have to tell you? You're *not* pushing me. And for the record, you think you can come live in LA and us not live together?"

"Noah... I..."

"I want to wake up every morning with you beside me. I want to go to bed every night and make fucking love to you."

"I'll have no time for yoga."

"That's okay. I heard if you sit on top reverse cowgirl, it's kind of the same thing."

Shaking my head, laughter escapes me. "Did Eric tell you that?"

"Sadly, yes."

"Noah, are you sure? How about Jessa and Nash? What'll Morgan say?"

There are so many questions, questions that need answering.

"I'll take care of Morgan. You shouldn't be concerned about her. Jessa will love to have you around. Nash doesn't even know where his nose is yet. Just say yes, Kate, say you'll come. Please."

"Yes... Noah. Yes." I grin hopelessly.

"You've made me the happiest man alive."

"Hmm..." I start removing my tank top, moving toward the shower. "I think I can make you happier."

I can hear the smirk smothering his face even though we can't see each other. "I bet you can. Shall I switch us to video call?"

"You know me too well, Mr. Mason."

TWENTY-TWO

KATE

I t's full steam ahead with my transition to LA.

Lex wants me full-time in the States within eight weeks. Easier said than done—I need to haul some serious ass.

Javier is taking over my role in Paris, and unfortunately for him, he has been paired with a much older personal assistant. I know he'd have gladly worked with Emile, given his interest in her during several corporate functions, but I wasn't going to let her go. I offered her a role as my assistant in LA, which she is ecstatic about. All she needs to do is say goodbye to her French boyfriend, Louis, and pack her bags to join me.

With so many things happening at one time, the days become a constant blur. Emile is tasked with packing up my apartment, along with organizing my belongings to be shipped to the States. It turns out I've accumulated more clothes and accessories than I thought, which prompts a significant wardrobe cull.

It's meeting after meeting until Lex calls and wants me to fly over for a quick introduction with the new team. It's supposed to be for only three days, and despite my heavy workload here, I only agree so I can see Noah. It's been six weeks of built-up sexual frustration, which video calls simply can't satisfy.

As I land in LAX, previously my most hated airport in the world, I welcome its chaos with open arms. Everything feels exactly the same as last time, yet completely different.

Setting foot on American soil means I'm this much closer to touching Noah.

It's early morning, and I'm not due in the office until lunchtime. I choose to hire a car this time due to the jam-packed schedule I have planned for the next three days, some of which involve off-site meetings.

Knowing that Noah is busy with work, which he doesn't argue the fact, I drive over to Charlie's place since she's working from home today. I desperately need a shower to wash off the plane smell and look presentable when meeting everyone at the new office.

"You're here!" Charlie runs outside with Addison following her. "Soon, I won't have to greet you with such enthusiasm."

We hug each other tightly before Addison demands my attention. Of all the three girls, she's the only one who looks like Charlie only because of the color of her mousy brown hair. They all possess Lex's green eyes, which Charlie often jokes about him definitely being their father. The joke, while humorous, never sits well with Lex.

I head straight for the shower, scrubbing away the awful travel smell, and then change into my ivory silk blouse and black pencil skirt. Beneath the skirt, I wear my garters and pantyhose, coupled with my Christian Louboutins. I plan to change into a different outfit for my date with Noah tonight

—some restaurant in Malibu which will hopefully end with some much-needed sex.

It's been that long, and there's only so much a woman do to help herself.

Before heading to the office, I want to make one pit stop. It has weighed heavily on my mind since our altercation at Amelia's party, and I know that I'm hugely to blame for what happened. Admitting my mistakes isn't my greatest strength, yet losing a close friend is not something I want to happen either.

My knuckles tap on the door. Minutes later, Eric opens it, dressed in a sharp gray suit.

"Oh." He eyes me dubiously before glancing aside. "It's you."

"Can I come in, please?"

With his mouth set in a hard line and arms crossed, he motions for me to follow him inside. Eric's condo is modern with gorgeous views of the Hollywood Hills. He lives here with Tristan, who has become this mega movie star. Who would have figured? The two of them an unlikely couple, yet they never can stay apart.

"I brought this for you." I hand him a white box with a red bow, gesturing for him to take it.

Using his perfectly manicured fingers, Eric opens the box and sifts through the tissue paper to pull out a mustard paisley cravat from a French boutique. The three elements he despises—the color mustard, paisley print, and, of course, the ever-so-controversial cravat.

"I wanted to say I'm sorry. For lying to you."

"By giving me a cravat?"

I nod, smiling, knowing how much he hates them. "If I'm honest, I was ashamed. I knew from the beginning it was wrong, but I let myself believe that I was a big girl, and I could handle it."

Eric releases a breath, staring at the box before raising his eyes to meet mine with a hopeless gaze. "Come here, give me a hug."

In Eric's embrace, the world feels right again. I've called him a drama queen, a pain in the ass, but the truth is, my life isn't complete without him in it.

"I'm sorry, too, for flat out calling you a whore. It just caught me by surprise. I seriously thought it was a joke when he told me."

"I wish it was."

"You got to him, you know," Eric confesses, keeping his voice low. "My whole life, we've barely spoken two words. It's like I was never good enough to be his little brother. But now it's all changed. It feels like we're family."

"I'm sorry," I repeat, then pressing my lips together thoughtfully. "But it was never going to work out between us. Two different people and two different lives."

"I know," he admits, running his hand against the fabric of the cravat. "And look, he'll move on. But he did... oh sorry... he does, love you."

Dominic has no idea what love means. But who am I to care anymore? It's a moot point, and my life is now with a man who loves me unconditionally. Dominic will move on, just like we all do when the stars don't align.

"I have ten minutes to catch up before meeting Lex at the office. Tell me, what's new with you?"

"Tristan and I took up hiking. Do you know how many hot French hikers we run into at the trail? I'm just waiting for an orgy to break out in the wilderness. You've got to teach me how to speak French."

"Well, if it's going to happen, then fingers crossed it's to you. You can call the video *Bareback Mountain*."

Eric snorts, followed by a ripple of laughter as I break out as well, unable to control myself until I fall into a coughing fit.

As we both try to calm down, Eric removes the cravat from the box entirely. "Let's say, for the sake of argument, I wore this one day. On a scale of one to ten, how many honey daddies would I score?"

I shake my head with a wide grin. Some things never change. "Ten. They'd be throwing themselves at you."

We speak a little bit more before I check the time and have to leave. I promise to catch up once I'm back permanently. In an odd expression, Eric looks rather pleased with himself, chewing his bottom lip with a knowing smirk. To add to that, his lingering silence also raises concern, but I've no choice but to ignore him for now.

Leaving his building, I welcome the short drive to the office to prepare myself for a very tiring few days.

Lex walks me through the building, introducing me to a few key people I'll be working with. I've forgotten how strong the American accent is, having been away for a while. According to many, I still have my British accent, though my linguistic efforts have been directed to learning French.

The building is rather large and modern, fifteen floors to be exact, in which we occupy all of them. It's located on Wilshire Boulevard in the heart of Beverly Hills, with Rodeo Drive just a few blocks away.

I've gone over the briefs, familiarized myself with our chain of hotels, and rise to the challenge Lex set, but nevertheless, the man will continue to push me because that's what he does best.

"Many of these hotels are outdated, the turnover is returning guests, but we're not capturing the new generation—the influencers with their self-made money to spend. We're talking complete overhaul, Lex, money spent on improving structures, expanding buildings, offering state-of-the-art amenities. Global campaigning is costly. This isn't an easy sell unless we've got the product to back it up."

"I agree, which is why I was able to secure the DeLuxe Group for a low amount. The board was tired, and they're ready to move on. And they don't have the funds to invest. I know we can bring this to where it needs to be, and I've given you the strongest team."

The board room opens with a man and a woman walking in. The man will be easily in his early thirties, and the lady, more mature at possibly fifty-odd.

"Rebecca is head of Finance, and Austin is our Chief of Information Technology."

I shake both of their hands, welcoming the two of them before asking them to take a seat. Another five people walk in, all of who are different heads of departments. Further to that, three of our shareholders also join us. We shake hands and exchange names. Luckily for me, I have a great memory when it comes to names.

Lex bows his head before Eric walks into the room. I shift my gaze to Lex, waiting for him to say something. "Eric Kennedy, Public Relations Manager."

Eric extends his hand with a professional smile. "Lovely to meet you, Miss Hamilton."

"Public relations?"

"Yes, Eric has been working on some side projects with me for quite some time, much to my wife's displeasure."

I keep my laugh at bay. Who would've thought Eric has something to do with public relations? Though, on further thought, he's born to do this role. I'm just surprised Lex hired him, having never alluded to this and given Charlie has mentioned that he is the glue that holds her business together on more than one occasion.

"So, this is the West Coast team?" I ask, smiling politely at everyone in the room.

"No, I have one more important person to introduce. In fact, someone you'll be working very closely with."

I look at Lex, then Eric, as he clasps his hands with a mischievous smile. "Our Chief Executive Officer."

With a company so large, I'd need a management team strongly suited. With some of Lex's larger endeavors, he hired a President and CEO. Fingers crossed I don't get some asshole on a power trip who will make my life hell. Surely, Lex knows how I operate and what I won't tolerate.

My eyes wander to the black Givenchy leather shoes which have stepped into the room. Slowly, they lift to the tailored slim-fit navy trousers and linger around the waist. My breathing stills, sweat building in the palm of my hands, although the air conditioning is turned up to cool the room.

Swallowing the lump caught in my throat, I bite my lip unwillingly as I continue to move upward past the white shirt and stop just where his chest is exposed—two buttons down. A thirst escapes me, the heat between my thighs rising as I make the final glance until I'm met with the eyes of *Noah*.

I am rendered speechless as he moves closer, extending his hand.

"Noah Mason," he introduces, his stare burning through me like an uncontrollable blaze.

I place my hand in his, the touch of his skin sending my

complete body into meltdown, a slight shiver escaping me. Unbeknownst to everyone in the room, his gaze shifts toward my mouth, causing him to bite his bottom lip unknowingly.

I clear my throat. "Kate Hamilton."

He releases his shake, taking a seat across from me, a playful smirk making it all the more uncomfortable to sit down given he's practically made me soaking wet with a simple hand gesture.

"Psst." Eric leans over, keeping his voice low as others take a seat. "Are you guys going to have the hottest sex tonight because the sexual tension in here is smoking hot?"

Eric has *no* idea how hot it will be.

And that will be my challenge for the rest of the day, ignoring just how sexy Noah is and anticipating exactly what he'll do to me tonight once we're alone.

Five hours later, and several American coffees consumed, everyone leaves the room with another meeting scheduled for tomorrow. There's much to absorb, my mind riddled with information, but the biggest question on the forefront of my mind is how Noah kept this from me.

Lex taps his pen on the table, switching his stare between Noah and me.

"I assume your personal relationship is here to stay?"

"Smart man," Noah chides, leaning back in his chair.

"Good," Lex states before playing with the band on his finger. "Off the record, I'm happy to see you two together. You're family to us. I wish you both a lifetime of happiness."

"Calm down, Lex." I shake my head while laughing. "It sounds like you're toasting a wedding."

A smile lightens Noah's eyes as he taps his fingers on the table. "Is a certain someone, someone you're married to, trying to probe into our relationship?"

"I admit to nothing. Off the record, you know my wife can be a handful at times."

"Well, you tell my nosy cousin that we're happy. One step at a time, right?"

"One step at a time," I agree, sunnily.

"Well, good. I respect the two of you and wouldn't have offered you this position if I didn't think you were capable. I don't trust many people, but neither one of you have ever let me down."

Lex directs our conversation to the outcome of the meeting, setting out an agenda for tomorrow. Shortly after, he leaves the room, so just the two of us are remaining.

"So, was this your 'things in the pipeline' secret?" I use air quotes around the words.

Noah is still sitting across from me, looking as delicious as he did the moment he stepped in. "Yes, I didn't know how you would react. When it comes to working, you're a control freak."

"Yes, I am. But we have a bigger problem," I admit leaning forward, aware that my blouse has dropped, and Noah's eyes are drawn to my breasts like a moth to a flame. "So, you're telling me that I'm supposed to pretend like I haven't felt you inside me? All day long, I'm supposed to be near you and curb the desire to touch you?"

Noah's smirk does nothing to calm me down, nor does the lick of his lips.

"All day long," he drags. "Luckily, the day is nearly over."

Noah rises from his chair, and instantly my eyes gravitate toward the crotch of his pants where he's rock hard. Moving slowly toward me, he leans into my ear, his cock grazing against my arm. "As soon as we're alone, you're all mine."

I try to control my breathing as I head to my office to find a very excited Eric—the biggest splash of cold water I could've asked for.

"Okay, tell me everything! Blow job, quick ram up the backside?"

"Eric, Noah and I are professionals. Besides, I'll take both later. So, you and Public Relations? You sure you're up for it?"

"Darling, I can be anyone you want me to be."

"Oh, really?" I chuckle.

"Yes, now back to Noah. How big are we talking?"

I shake off the laugh, not answering his question and asking him respectfully to leave me alone, so I can make a call to the Paris office. After Eric leaves, I send Charlie a quick text.

Me: *I got Eric in our custody battle? I thought you wanted sole custody.*

Charlie: *Nah, he's too much hard work. I do best co-parenting.*

Noah changes plans for us, telling me to meet him at his place in one hour. I don't even have time to change or grab my things, knowing he left an hour ago with Lex to attend another meeting. He left a key for me with the receptionist, just in case he's running late.

I place the key in the lock and step inside the apartment to be met with all the lights turned off. Before I manage to find the switch, hands move around my waist before turning me around—the familiar scent engulfing me.

"Noah," I breathe.

He doesn't say a word, lifting my skirt and entering me

with a grunt. I gasp in his grip, moving in sync, our lips crashing against each other unable to get enough.

"You're such a tease, wearing this skirt, pursing your beautiful lips. How will I punish you for taunting me all day?"

My arm wraps around his neck, pulling him in, begging to go deeper. "Baby, you can't punish me. You want me too much."

I pull him out, sliding my back against the wall until I'm crouched, and his beautiful cock is in front of me. I take it all in, watching him arch his back until he wraps my hair around his hand and pushes me deeper, exploding inside of me. I move up as he inserts his fingers, my back pressing against the wall until a sudden flush of warmth spreads to every inch of my body, possessing me in a way only Noah can do.

My breaths are uneven, a rasp in my throat from my deep moans. I grip onto his shoulders to gain my balance and adjust my skirt as Noah cups my face, planting a loving kiss.

"I have to tell you something," he says, walking me to the bedroom where he strips my clothes off, leaving me completely naked—kissing my shoulder. "I knew Lex was offering you the position. He spoke to me first and, of course, I thought it was brilliant. He texted me after he spoke to you."

"Is that why you were quiet when I called you?"

"I was afraid you would say no."

"I'll admit I had to think about it, not because I didn't want to be with you but because I needed to make sure I was strong enough to be the person you need me to be."

"And are you?" he asks, inches away from me.

"With you in my bed every night, I'm Wonder-fucking-Woman."

He carries me in his arms, laying me on the bed as we make love all night long to the sounds of the waves crashing against the shoreline.

Another perfect night in the arms of the man I love.

I always knew three days would fly by so quickly. Work commitments have me occupied. Luckily, Noah is in on every meeting, so I get to still see him even though it's on a professional level. Since I haven't worked with him before, to see him command the room is something else. I have to keep reminding myself to focus and not think about him completely naked buried between my thighs.

We do, however, have a strong management team. There are a few roles we still need to hire for which Lex left to us, but all in all, I'm pleased with the skillset each person possesses and feel confident about reaching our set targets with global domination insight.

Our company owns and funds many larger hotel chains across the States, meaning travel is imminent. Our team put together a short-term itinerary, which means both Noah and I will be traveling separately to different places over the next few months. The silver lining to all of this is that although we will spend some days apart, we'll have more time together than if I stayed in Paris.

On my last night, we lay in bed all night long, relishing the moment before my early flight.

"I wish you didn't have to leave."

"It's not for long," I remind him while caressing his arm. "I'll be back in three weeks for good."

"I know. But I'm selfish and want you now."

"Good things come to those who wait."

"Speaking of good things, I was thinking—"

"It's never good when you're thinking," I interrupt him with a smile playing on my lips. "It can end up with us in a jail cell again or me taking it back door outside on your balcony."

"Hmm... dirty mind, Miss Hamilton. I was just thinking about how beautiful you'll look spread out with your ass ready for me." His lips find me again, but he pulls away, leaving me breathless. "But that isn't it. I was thinking, this place isn't big enough for us. It's a fair distance from the office, and I don't want to spend my time on the road when I can be here with you."

"You want to move to where?"

"Us to move." He looks deep into my eyes. "Something bigger, a room for Jessa when she stays and one for Nash."

"Wait, back up. Nash? Has something happened?"

"Olivia agreed to move to LA. I pitched your idea, and she's managed to find a local job. You know, she'd love to meet you... her words, not mine."

"I... I'd love to meet her, too. I mean, if Nash is going to stay with us some days, I guess I need to get to know her, right?"

"I'd love for you to but no pressure."

"I've just never been around kids much, aside from Charlie's."

"One day at a time. We're still trying to put together a schedule, and I want you to be part of this."

I pull the sheet over me, my chest hitching as the room begins to heat up. "Noah, I... this is a lot, okay? I've never had to factor kids in, ever."

"I know it's a lot. But we're together now, and soon you'll be my wife so..."

"Um... hold up. Your wife?"

"Where did you think our relationship would lead?"

"I don't know... I didn't think about marriage," I sputter, momentarily beyond words, while trying to digest this all. "I just thought about us being together, and that's it."

"Okay, well, here's the thing. I'm in love with you, and I refuse to let you go again. I want a future with you. I want to call you my wife, one day, apparently the day you stop freaking out over it..."

I smack a pillow in his face. The overwhelming feeling fades, and the realization of his pure intentions bring a welcoming smile. "You've just caught me by surprise. And besides, as if I could ever say no to you."

Noah angles his head, brushing his lips against my mouth in a soft kiss. "I'm charming. It's one of the only things I have going for me."

"Uh-uh. That's not true. You also have beautiful lips and nice hair." My hand wanders between his legs where he is rock hard. "And the most perfect cock in the world."

"Hmm," he moans. "According to Eric, it's supposed to be Orlando Bloom."

I climb on top of him, sliding myself on. "You've got five hours left to show me just how perfect it is."

"Oh, baby," Noah groans, bucking his hips. "Get ready."

Like he has always done, Noah makes me forget that the entire world exists, and the only thing on my mind is him.

Saying goodbye is hard but knowing I'll be back forever, changes my outlook. We agree to go house hunting upon my return, our first step to cementing our relationship. Although Noah makes it known that he has little patience for architecture, if I brought up the words 'meticulous craftsmanship' or 'wainscotting,' he said he'd swap him out for Eric.

A typical male and lucky for him, I love architecture and design. So does Eric.

I decide to keep my apartment in Paris, renting it out to someone who works at Lexed. In ways, it feels like I'm giving up everything I've ever known, but I welcome this new journey because it's time to live my happily ever after.

I even connected with Olivia on Facebook. She's actually pretty easy-going, and one day, she calls me to chat. I can see why Noah is more relaxed with her. Olivia is very rational and wants to get together when I come home. She also asks about how comfortable I will be in Nash's life. Given that I haven't met him, I don't know exactly how to respond, but I suggest we talk more when I get back.

As for Morgan, Noah says she won't be easy. It isn't about another woman being in Noah's life.

It's *me*.

The woman who she believes has always owned Noah's heart.

I know this *will* be a battle, and one I have no idea how to conquer. So, for now, unlike Olivia, who welcomes me into her son's life with open arms, I'm yet to have any communication with Morgan Bentley.

The biggest hurdle is yet to come—meet face to face with the woman who hates me most of all.

A scorned ex-wife who holds her cards close to her chest, ready to strike at any moment.

But before I embark on what'll be my greatest journey yet, I have to say goodbye to one of my greatest loves—Paris.

Standing on my balcony as I've done many times before, I take it all in from every angle possible. The cool air and soft breeze rustle with the leaves falling on the sidewalk.

Warm, earth-tone colors replace the blossoming flowers with the hint of winter upon us.

This city—romantic, magical, in a league of its own—will always be my first true love.

I've rediscovered who I am and have allowed myself to explore things outside of my normally controlled comfort zone. I've been bold with my choices, yet disciplined when faced with challenges. And I've learned that the most cherished memories you'll ever make are with the person you love.

Paris taught me how to fall in love.

With a place, my best friend, and most importantly, myself.

"*Au revoir mon amour*," I whisper in the autumn night. "Until next time."

TWENTY-THREE

KATE

Noah loves his toys.

When I say toys, I mean his Lexus.

His other baby.

"Listen, I'm not a car enthusiast like yourself, but when are too many cars too many cars?"

Noah keeps his eyes on the road, shifting gears as he drives up the steep street.

"You can never have enough."

"But explain to me again why you want to look at the house with the four garages when you only have one car?"

"Correction... I have a motorcycle, too."

"Okay, so that's two."

"And there are the boat and jet ski..." he trails off.

"You have a boat and a jet ski? What else have you been hiding?"

The corners of his mouth lift. "Nothing yet. But I do love water sports."

"Well, I'm English, so our water sports consist of watching crazy-minded people swim the English Channel. I also should sort out my own car soon. Care to go shopping for me because I couldn't think of anything worse."

"A mini-van? Because you know, once we actually have kids, you'll have to cart them around to soccer games. Living the mom life."

I keep my smile fixed. Noah enjoys pushing my buttons just to goad me. That much is evident when I see him side-eye me with an annoying smirk on his face.

"You know, maybe, I hear soccer moms get bored with their workaholic husbands. Always away at the office. Before you know it, I'll be binge-reading romance novels when the kids are at school waiting for the plumber to arrive," I tease, watching his face fall. "Oh, wait, or is that a carpenter? I can never remember who wears the short shorts with the tanned-colored work boots."

"Okay, jokes over. I like you in the office where I can keep my eye on you."

I lean back in the seat with a satisfied smile and admire the large houses we drive past.

I've only been here for a few days when Charlie springs on me a place not too far from hers which just came on the market. They are motivated sellers, something about a nasty divorce and a wandering pussy. Charlie's words—not mine.

Noah agrees, but the only time we can fit it in is today during lunch. It should've been a quick trip if Noah didn't insist on taking a detour because he claims he's suffering blue balls.

Despite my arguing that not only did we have sex for four straight hours last night, we also snuck in some anal in the shower this morning. He continues to amaze me with his stamina, something I thought I could keep up with but clearly, I'm drained. Adjusting to the time zone becomes more problematic than I thought, my body still on Parisian time. Nevertheless, he got the blow he desperately craved on some abandoned street near a hiking trail.

Noah pulls up to the house as we hop out of the car and greet the realtor.

The house is privately gated, English Tudor nestled within the historic Santa Monica mountains. It has six bedrooms, five baths, large living areas, plus a gourmet kitchen. Noah holds my hand as we walk through, and I bite my tongue to stop myself from commenting on the wainscoting.

There's a large study area should either one of us need to work from home. The more I see the property, the more I fall in love with it.

The realtor takes us to the master bedroom, where our eyes are immediately drawn to the tacky mirrored ceiling. I turn to look as he does the same.

"You would think," I whisper. "If you had these mirrors, the wife's pussy didn't need attention elsewhere."

Noah bows his head, chuckling softly beside me. "It's awful, but I think it's the selling point of this house."

I nudge him with my elbow, knowing all too well that if we buy this house, Noah will not take them down.

Outside is a sprawling backyard with a luscious green lawn, a large pool with spa on the side, a basketball court, plus striking views of rolling hills and scenic mountain ranges, making it the perfect location.

"So, what do you think?" the realtor asks, looking hopeful.

"It's a nice property," I tell him, keeping my expression fixed. "We'll have a talk and get back to you soon."

I shake his hand, prompting our exit, not giving any indication of how I truly feel because that's the first sign of weakness. Negotiation is a strong trait of mine, and there's not a chance in hell we'll pay their asking price.

Inside the car, I turn to Noah. "What do you think?"

"That you're a shark with excellent negotiation skills."

"I mean about the house."

"It's beautiful, it has everything we need, but to be honest, I don't care as long as you're by my side."

"Cue the romantic talk, Mason," I huff with a playful smile. "But did you see the wainscoting?"

Noah covers his face with his hands, releasing a groan. "Enough with the wainscoting. I don't care about that. If you love it, it's ours."

I do love it. I love it too much. Charlie knew I'd love it, and because Charlie loves it, and we have similar tastes, I know this will be the one.

"I don't want to give Richard an offer just yet. The sellers are motivated. I did a little snooping, and a large percentage of this sale will go to the pussy cheater. So, the jilted husband will accept lower just to get her back."

"How do you even know all this?"

"Don't underestimate my power, baby."

Noah's phone buzzes between us. He reaches to grab it, reading the text with a concerned expression on his face.

"What's wrong?"

"It's Morgan. She has to fly out tonight for a last-minute meeting and asked if I can have Jessa all weekend."

It's supposed to be our first weekend together in which we have no plans but to lay in bed and watch Netflix. Keeping my expression stilled, I press my lips thoughtfully together to curb my disappointment.

"Is that okay?" he adds, eyeing me dubiously.

"Of course, she's your daughter. You never have to ask."

"I know, but it's our first weekend."

"Listen, we'll have fun. So, Morgan knows, right?"

Noah rubs his neck, wincing while avoiding eye contact.

"Oh, bloody hell," I berate, my British slang tumbling out in sheer frustration. "*Vous êtes* impossible!"

"Hey!" Noah scoffs, his face hardening. "Pick a language, will you? I'm not impossible. I told her you moved to the States and that we're in a relationship."

"But?"

"I just left out the part of you living with me..." he trails off in a softer tone.

I throw my head back into the seat, annoyed at his resistance to finally tell her the whole truth. "You need to grow some balls and tell her."

"I have balls, thank you very much," he notes in dark amusement. "In fact, you loved them in your mouth only an hour ago. I'll tell her, I promise."

"Well, you're running out of time, buddy. Jessa will come over tonight, and what would you like me to do, magically disappear all weekend?"

"No," he states firmly. "I'll sort this out today."

The ride to the office is quiet, each one of us keeping our thoughts to ourselves. It dampens my mood, and after we go our separate ways, I receive a text from Noah during an afternoon conference call.

Noah: *It's done.*

I should've felt relieved, no more hiding our relationship, but it isn't enough. I know that if I'm to be around Jessa and help Noah co-parent, I need to speak to Morgan face to face. I don't want to always be communicating through Noah because, let's face it, men can be hopeless at times.

Pressing dial on my phone, I let my temporary assistant know that I'll be stepping out of the office for an hour. Grabbing my things, I remember that we drove to work in one car. *Shit.* Thinking quickly, I order an Uber and hope that the address I have is correct, and most importantly, Morgan is at her office.

Clutching my purse beneath my arm, I step into the fancy building and make my way to the receptionist's desk. The red-headed bimbo with her obvious hair extensions plasters a fake smile as I ask for Morgan.

"She's not taking appointments right now."

"Well, perhaps if you give her my name, I'm certain she'll see me."

The young girl, clueless and a waste of office space, dials her number, bowing her head until she hangs up.

"Follow me."

I walk behind her, noting her dress is way too short to be acceptable in the workplace. But this isn't my office.

Stopping at the door, she ushers me in as my eyes meet Morgan's from across the table.

"You may leave, Tiffany."

I purse my lips, standing in place. "May I take a seat?"

Morgan remains silent. I sit down on the white leather chair, crossing my legs as my eyes gravitate toward her pictured frame of Jessa on her desk.

"I'd like to make it clear that Noah didn't send me here, nor is he aware that I am here."

Morgan looks perplexed, but beneath it, I see the eyes of a woman who has zero empathy for me right now.

"Then why are you here?"

"Noah has told you of our relationship and our living situation?"

"Why, yes." She releases a disturbing laugh. "It's all very last minute, isn't it? I tell him I need to go away and ask if he can take Jessa, then he throws this giant curveball in my face like I'm not supposed to care."

"I understand your concern."

"Do you?" She stands, moving closer to the window to create distance between us. The red body-con dress she wears molds to her figure perfectly, matching the shade of lipstick applied to her full lips. "Do you understand what it's like to be a mother of two children, one with special needs? And to have your husband bounce from woman to woman?"

"From memory, Michael came into your life, and you welcomed him with open arms, correct? You loved his father and made sacrifices to be the best stepmother you could be," I inform her, trying to drive my point home but attempting to keep my tone controlled. "So, while I don't have any biological children, I do believe in the power of love. I understand what it's like to be loved by a parent. My role in Noah's life is not to replace you. You're irreplaceable. I'm his best friend, his partner, and his family is everything to him. As for the bouncing woman-to-woman comment, nobody is perfect. Noah isn't, I'm not, and I'm pretty sure you aren't either."

"That's the first time I've ever heard that," she mumbles, lowering her head. "Because I'm being made to feel like I am irreplaceable."

"You're Jessa's mother and always will be. Nothing could ever change that. I'm only asking that we work together as a team. We all want the same thing, for Jessa to be happy and feel the love she so greatly deserves."

"And what about Michael? He's grown fond of Noah. Noah has always been this male figure in his life. I can't take that away from him."

"He's welcome in our home, Morgan," I insist, my eyes watching her closely. "You don't have to do any of this alone. Just remember that."

Silence falls between us, and despite my phone blowing up with notifications, I don't want to push her. I don't want any animosity between us, worried it will filter through to the little girl who's innocent in all of this.

"I knew, from the beginning, that you and Noah had this unbreakable bond. I should've followed my instincts."

"I know exactly how it feels to be on the outside looking in. I'm not here to flaunt our relationship. I truly want to make this work. And while you may not trust me around your daughter, I hope, with time, you'll feel comfortable enough to do so."

I check my watch while standing. "I appreciate your time today."

As I turn to leave the room, Morgan calls my name.

"Jessa likes to read at night. Her favorite is *Beauty and the Beast* like her cousin, Addison."

I nod my head with a knowing smile.

"She's obsessed with unicorns right now, so if she doesn't eat her food, tell her that unicorns eat all their food so they can fly."

"Seems logical." I nod again.

"And Noah always spoils her when they go out. If you can try to control his urge to buy her every stuffed toy known to man, I'd appreciate it."

"I'm happy to crack the whip and control his spoiling of stuffed toys."

I release a sigh, keeping my stare fixated on Morgan.

"It'll work out, this whole co-parenting thing. We simply have to find the rhythm, so we can play the right chords."

I turn back around, leave the room, and head back to the office.

When I step inside my office, Noah is standing at the window, arms folded and his brows snapped together with an unrelenting stare. He's removed his jacket he wore earlier on, wearing only his white business shirt with a herringbone blue vest and matching pants. His tanned belt and shoes match. The guy knows how to dress, making it harder to resist him. He screams *sexy* even when he's staring at you with angered eyes.

"Where were you?"

"I went to see Morgan."

"You met with Morgan?"

"Yes."

"And?" His eyes widen, hands moving toward his pockets in anticipation. "You're alive?"

Moving over to where he stands, I grab his hand and place it on my heart. "Yes, still beating."

"Is that all you're going to say?"

I explain to him what happened, knowing his pride and ego will have an opinion, but I've learned how to make him see the bigger picture and not focus on what isn't worth his time. His fear of losing his kids often makes his reaction reactive.

"It's not that easy, everything you're offering."

"Life isn't easy, Noah," I remind him sternly. "We've said from the beginning that our relationship will be unlike others. Granted, your baggage is bigger than mine... I only bring Eric."

"I don't know. I'd argue who's is bigger."

"Do you trust me?"

"Of course, I do." He softens.

"Then, we can do this together, okay?"

He nods, sliding his hands back into his pockets, knowing all too well our office protocol, and touching each other is off-limits.

"So, what time are you picking up Jessa? And, what do you want to do this weekend?"

"Hmm, I was thinking of a movie tonight. Chances are it's *Beauty and the Beast* for like the hundredth time. Then tomorrow, we hit up Santa Monica Pier. She loves all the stuffed bears."

The corners of my mouth quirk up.

"Why are you smiling like that?"

"Oh, nothing," I say, with a surge of happiness. "Just something between Morgan and me. You know, secret women's business."

I half expect him to beg me to tell him, but instead, he crosses his arms, giving me that sexy stare he always does. "It is happening already. I guess it's going to be two against one, huh?"

"Three against one, honey, you forgot about Olivia," I so eagerly remind him. "Aren't I lucky to have fallen in love with you?"

"The luckiest woman in the world." He chuckles softly before his expression turns hopeful. "You know how grateful I am, right?"

"Yeah," I shrug my shoulders with a playful smirk. "I guess so. But it won't hurt you to show me later, you know, once Jessa is asleep."

Noah licks his lips before leaning in to whisper, "You'll have to be as quiet as a mouse. Think you can handle that?"

"I'm always up for a challenge, Mr. Mason."

TWENTY-FOUR

KATE

It was exactly this time twelve months ago when I enjoyed a magnificent dinner at Benoit.

The restaurant is one of the most expensive dining experiences in Paris, where the food is exquisite, and they treat you like you're the only patron dining.

On that lonely Christmas Eve after a year of working nonstop, it was a gift to me from me. I can recall how enjoyable the experience had been, though never truly understanding the depth of my loneliness since I had distracted myself with a once-in-a-lifetime experience.

It was also a time in my life when I thought I had it figured out, only to look back now and realize how miserable I had been.

I just never imagined my life taking such a drastic turn, for the better, of course.

I stare at my list, ticking off the tasks completed. The last two months have been nothing but madness. We put an offer in on the house, and thanks to my negotiation skills, we got the place at a steal. I could've sworn I saw the scorned husband smoking a cigar as he walked away, satisfied he'd equally screwed his pussy-cheating wife over.

With that came the tedious task of moving. Noah's place in Malibu is your typical bachelor pad. Minimalist modern furniture with no character. So, of course, I have the enjoyable task of furnishing our new place. Noah bailed out, saying that he doesn't care what I do as long as the mirrors stayed.

The mirrors are hideous.

But I pick my battles, and frankly, they become very useful during sex.

It was Charlie and Eric to the rescue. We spent hours on Pinterest, putting together mood boards, and trying to source pieces before Christmas. Some are local, others have to be imported. Since I'm trying to put together our first family home, every detail matters.

Between work, some traveling to Colorado, and moving houses, I barely have time for anything else. Naturally, Noah has something to say because the man is greedy, wanting me naked every moment I'm at home.

"Phone down," he warns me, though his eyes hover on his phone sitting beside him.

"But wait. I have to get the address for this place Charlie and I are going to on Saturday to pick up an end table."

"An end table?"

"Yes, it will be the perfect piece next to the couch beside that dead space, which, by the way, is driving me crazy."

Noah pinches the bridge of his nose, trying to calm his frustration. "Is it possible, for just one night, that I can have you focused on me? You know, your charming manfriend with the killer abs and, according to you, the biggest cock you've ever seen."

I place my phone down, turning to face him. "I'm focused on you, manfriend."

Noah scans my face, his eyes creasing. "No, you are not. You're thinking about which lamp will go on the end table, am I right?"

"Listen here, a lamp positioned correctly can change the whole dynamic of the room."

"I need to shove something in your mouth to shut you up. I have an idea just what..."

Ripping the sheets away, his already naked body kneels in front of me where I have no choice but to focus on what's in front of me.

And yes, it's the most beautiful, biggest, most perfect cock I have ever seen.

It's fair to say that living with Noah isn't as easy as I thought. We argue over many things. He's a control freak, and so am I, but over different things. We disagree on food and certain brands, making grocery shopping a battle I'd rather not face with him.

He blames my stubborn English background for always complaining about how hot it is in LA, and although it's winter, I crank up the air conditioning when he argues it is freezing cold.

Our 'Netflix and Chill' nights have become just Chill nights. Noah only agrees to watch my movies because he knows it always leads to sex in the first ten minutes when he gets bored. By the time we're done, we've lost half the movie, and I have to rewind and start all over again, much to his displeasure.

Even though we officially live together, our schedules

are chaotic. We both have demanding roles, with his requiring a bit more travel. In the past week alone, he's flown to Phoenix and Seattle. Even at the office, our roles vary, so we barely see each other unless a meeting calls for the entire management team.

It works in our favor that each of us understands our work commitments. I never once complain about his attention to being elsewhere, knowing all too well the demands and responsibilities of both our roles.

My position has been a challenge for me and a vast difference from my role in France. The biggest hurdle, once again, is adjusting to American culture. Thankfully, Emile flew over a month ago and became my saving grace. Much like Lex and I, Emile has become part of the well-oiled machine we run. Despite her being French and new to the States, she knows how to perform as a personal assistant, which is all that matters.

And, of course, to add to the stress of work and doing our best to create a balance, we have the kids to think about.

Jessa is easy. You can play anything with her, and time will just pass. Nash, on the other hand, needs constant attention. In my wildest dreams, I never envisioned my life with children. It's a lot to handle, but thankfully, Noah is an amazing father and takes the stress off me. He makes it look easy and never admonishes me for asking a thousand questions I have on how to take care of them.

When they stay with us, I'll be completely exhausted by the end of the night, barely able to make it to bed with my eyes open. Not even Noah can tire me out with his insatiable sex drive, and that's saying a lot.

Most of the house is now furnished, including the kids' rooms. Jessa and I had a day out to pick all her things. She loves unicorns, so we make it a unicorn-themed room with a giant rainbow mural on her wall. As for Nash, since Noah loves basketball, we made it sports themed. I'll admit, furnishing those two rooms were my favorite part of all of this.

We even set up our guest room for Michael on the rare occasion he stays, but over the last year, according to Noah, he's spent a lot of time with his biological mother, who lives in San Diego.

Today marks our first official Christmas Eve.

I've rushed around town all day, trying to finish present shopping. The stores are chaotic, last-minute shoppers like me with zero courtesy for anyone else. I hate to admit it, but the feisty Brit in me came out on several occasions.

The house is decorated, the large tree is in the corner with all the presents neatly piled underneath, and garland is wrapped around our large staircase. Before the guests arrive, I take a moment to take it all in. Our home is beautiful, and I can't be prouder.

Adriana is the first to arrive with Julian and the kids. She stays in the kitchen with me as we chat while preparing the food. I've never cooked to this level and enlisted everyone's help because I feel out of my element.

When it comes to discussing my relationship with Noah, Adriana has been my go-to, given that Charlie doesn't want to hear about her cousin ravaging me in bed.

"I just thought, you know, after a few months, he'd tire out, but here we are."

"Uh-huh, tell me more?" Adriana grins with a glass of wine in her hand.

"He's insatiable. I mean, I know we have busy schedules, and he's had to travel, and so have I, but when we're together..."

"Oh, really? Go on..." she urges, eyes wide with curiosity.

"I thought working together would be hard. That we couldn't separate our personal life from work, but we actually don't see each other too much. We're either off-site or in meetings, but then we see each other in the elevator and..."

"*And?*"

"I have no words."

"Of course, you have words!"

I chuckle softly beside her while chopping carrots. "Hey, you have yourself a gorgeous man. Surely, you don't have to live vicariously through me?"

"Yes, I have a beautiful husband, but we also have the two biggest cockblockers known to man."

"Charlie warned me about this."

"Don't even start with Charlie and my brother. Those two are like rabbits. But you guys have the best of both worlds, one week to yourselves and one week with the kids. Isn't that perfect?"

"It suits everyone. Olivia took a job at Burbank Airport, so her hours are stable. Noah's mom, Naomi, watches Nash two days a week, and the other three he's in daycare. Depending on the days, Noah and I take turns picking him up."

"And Jessa?"

"She started pre-school, so we do the same. She loves spending time with Nash, dotes on him like crazy."

"How does it feel to be an instant mum, especially to a baby?"

"Noah is great. He's born to be a father. I'm still learning. I don't know how you do it."

"Julian is great, too. He is so hands-on, and without him, I'd go insane. He's that calm, and I'm the storm." She laughs, watching Julian outside with Noah and the kids. "But you're amazing. You're the glue that holds your non-conventional family together. Both Julian and I learned that family doesn't mean you have to carry a baby for nine months. It comes in all shapes and forms. I never expected to love a child so much who didn't have the same blood as me, but I can't imagine my life without Luna. She was always destined for our family."

"You guys have always inspired me. And Julian is great."

As soon as I say the words, Julian and Andy walk into the kitchen. Julian leans over to kiss Adriana on the cheek as Andy steals a piece of cheese from the platter.

"Dad, can we go play ball with Noah when Uncle Lex gets here?"

Julian shares a playful grin. "You think we can beat them?"

"We kicked their ass last time."

Adriana shakes her head with a heavy sigh. "Language, kid."

"Sorry, Mom. But it's true. They're all talk. Dad and I totally beat them."

Both Adriana and I let out a snicker. For an eight-year-old, Andy is quite tall, and it won't surprise me one bit if he grows to be taller than all the men. He absolutely loves sports. Such a boy's boy, which is fortunate for him since he has amazing men around him.

Lex and Charlie arrive with their family. The girls all run off to the backyard to play with the other kids. Lex goes outside to play ball with the boys while we finish preparing dinner.

"Kate, I can't believe you did all this. Remember that Thanksgiving at my place years ago when I had to show you how to open a can?" Charlie reminds me with a laugh. "You and Eric watched on, completely clueless."

"Oh, don't remind me. How is it even possible that I can close a multi-million-dollar deal but can't open a can of cranberry sauce?"

"So, no Eric?" Adriana questions.

"Not this time. Eric wants to formally introduce Tristan to his parents. They're in The Hamptons for the holidays."

"And Emile, did you invite her?"

"She flew back to Paris to spend Christmas with her family."

The doorbell continues to ring. Olivia arrives with baby Nash the same time Noah's mom, Naomi, arrives. Over the past few months, we've gotten to know each other more, and I swear, I love her. Naomi knows exactly how to put her son in place and is the extra support we need with the kids.

I offer to take the dish from Olivia's hands, but she smiles and declines. "Please take Mr. Poopy Pants out of his carrier instead. I'd change him, but he has managed to push all my buttons, literally. He touched my phone, and now it's all in *Japanese*."

Leaning in, I tickle his chubby little feet before unstrapping his belt. His innocent little giggles warm my heart as they have done a dozen times before. But, true to what Olivia just said, a foul odor needs attention.

I take him to his bedroom, changing his diaper before grabbing him a bottle and placing him in his crib since it's naptime according to my watch. It only takes him minutes to close his eyes before I close the door, leaving a small gap, and head back to the kitchen.

"It smells delicious, Kate," Olivia compliments, taking a glass of red from Adriana. "I can't even remember the last time I've been to a Christmas dinner. I was always working."

"Me, too." I laugh, raising my glass in the air. "Shall we toast?"

"Yes." She follows as does Adriana and Charlie. "*Salut!*"

Olivia and I are very similar. Much like me, she spent years away from family just working. Her chilled nature makes it easy to chat, and quite often, she comes over and has dinner with us. Noah is also relaxed around her, and although they only had one night of passion, the two of them communicate without the tension.

The doorbell rings again, so I excuse myself to answer.

Morgan is at the entrance with her new partner, Callum. He's a nice enough man, much older than her but polite and always attentive. According to Noah, he's a director, which is how Morgan met him through her sister, Scarlett.

Jessa runs up to me, wrapping her arms around my legs. "Kate, look what Mommy did to my hair?" She parades her cute pigtails.

"An excellent job. Your mommy is very talented."

Morgan hands me a bottle of wine while Callum balances a glazed ham looking oh so mouth-watering on a silver platter. "Thank you. Please come in."

Jessa lets go as Noah enters the room. She jumps into his arms, kissing his face. "Daddy, is baby Nash here? I want to show Mommy."

"He's sleeping, Jessa. But he'll wake up soon."

Olivia enters the foyer. Noah turns to me, apprehensive, but I give him a reassuring glance reminding him not to react. It's the first time Morgan and Olivia have officially met.

"Morgan, this is Olivia, Nash's mother," Noah introduces, politely.

Morgan's stare falls blank as does her silence. Callum extends his hand, introducing himself before Morgan smiles and shakes her hand as well.

Jessa comes bouncing down the stairs, disappearing during our awkward exchange.

"Nash is awake, Olivia! Can we please show my mommy?"

Noah offers to get him as I settle Morgan and Callum in the dining room with everyone else. Moments later, a happy little boy is sitting in Noah's arms.

"Hey, Nash, you want to meet your sister's mommy?"

He brings him closer to Morgan, and I give Olivia a reassuring smile. Through our open conversations, Olivia has always felt to blame for Noah's and Morgan's marriage ending. She never admitted that to Noah, but between us girls, I know the truth. I reassured her several times that their marriage had cracks well before Olivia, and that it didn't matter since a beautiful little boy came into this world, making it a much better place.

"He's beautiful, Noah." Morgan touches baby Nash's face with a soft glance.

"Hold him, Mommy!"

Morgan is resistant, but to please Jessa, she takes Nash from Noah's arms.

"Hello, little boy," she coos as Nash smiles infectiously.

She hands him back to Noah as Jessa demands Morgan see the Christmas tree and all the presents.

"The house is beautiful, Kate," Morgan praises while taking a glass of wine from Callum. "You've really done a lot since I last came here."

"It's been exhausting with work and the holidays, but it's slowly coming together."

"You have an eye for designing. I remember when we first bought our house, I couldn't even think about paint colors. I ended up calling Scarlett's interior designer to do it all."

Noah keeps his smile fixed. When it comes to Morgan, Noah's temper flares out of control at the drop of a hat. I've seen it on several occasions, and to be honest, they are just as bad as each other. I suspect the memory she so fondly shares isn't pleasant for him, hence his silence.

We gather around the table, all taking a seat as Noah suggests we say grace.

"Thank you for our family, for our blessings, our triumphs, and our health."

He opens his eyes and looks around until his eyes land on me. "They say it takes a village to raise a child, so thank you, Lord, for connecting our family and bringing us all here tonight."

"Amen," we all say in unison.

Our night is filled with children's laughter, the sound of Christmas carols, and the drinking of eggnog plus wine. The food tastes divine if I say so myself, and I don't think anyone will disagree since everyone helps themselves to seconds.

Gifts are exchanged, and scraps of wrapping paper are strewn around the tree as the kids open their presents in a mad rush.

As the evening wears on, Olivia calls it a night but has

the difficult task of leaving Nash with us since she has a shift commencing at dawn.

"I hate leaving him," she tells me. "Mommy guilt is real."

"Hey, it's okay. You'll be here for lunch tomorrow, right? Nash can open his presents from Santa then."

Olivia breathes a sigh of relief, holding onto me tight. "Thank you, Kate. For everything. I couldn't do this without you and Noah."

Releasing her from our embrace, I give her a knowing smile. "And thank you to you for bringing this beautiful boy into the world. Who else is going to wake me up at three in the morning because he lost his binky?"

Olivia laughs, placing her hand on my shoulder. "My Christmas gift is sleeping straight through tonight. I'll see you tomorrow."

Everyone else says their goodbyes, wishing each other a Merry Christmas, leaving only us with Morgan and Callum. Nash is long tired out, in bed, and fast asleep.

As I step back inside the house, I watch as Jessa shows Noah her gift, and Morgan sits beside them. I take a step back, allowing the three of them to have their moment. It isn't easy, seeing the man I love with his ex-wife and the family they created, but it isn't about me. It's about the little girl between them who deserves this memory.

And if life has taught me anything, it's to be patient and allow others to have their moments. Even if, occasionally, it makes me slightly uncomfortable.

When Jessa lets out a yawn, the excitement becomes all too much.

"This was... perfect, Kate," Morgan says while gathering her belongings. "You've made this all come together, and I'm in awe of you. For the longest time, I couldn't accept

Noah had created another family, but you've made this work. And Lord knows it mustn't have been easy when I made your life hell."

"It's okay," I reassure her. "I kinda think I was born to do it. Be a stepmom. Who would've thought?"

She places her hand on my arm. "As a stepmother myself, you're doing a fantastic job. Merry Christmas." And before she leaves, she leans in to hug Noah. "Merry Christmas, Noah."

I watch him stiffen, uncomfortable with the show of affection. But slowly, he relaxes and even offers a smile.

With everyone now gone, I head into the kitchen to clean up until Noah wraps his arms around my waist. "Stop... this can wait. I have something for you."

"Is it in your pants? Because no offense or anything, I've kind of peeked, so it isn't really a surprise."

"No," he drags, rolling his eyes. "Follow me."

Grabbing the last bottle of wine and two glasses along with the baby monitor, I follow him into the living room when he demands I sit. He pulls out a small black box and hands it to me. "Merry Christmas."

"I thought we said no presents till tomorrow?"

"This can't wait."

I open the black velvet box, and inside is a white gold necklace with two small pendants. One is a diamond-encrusted Eiffel Tower, and the other is a key.

"It's beautiful, Noah," I gush, removing it from the box as he places it around my neck and clasps the chain. My fingers wander to the pendants, playing with them and reminiscing about our time in Paris. "But what does the key mean?"

"It's a replica of the key to our chateau."

My mouth falls open. "Our chateau?"

"To quote you, 'Any home is a castle when the King and Queen are in love,'" he whispers, brushing his lips against my neck. "I made an offer on the chateau in Champagne. The one you fell in love with and couldn't stop gushing about. Now, before you say anything, I've spoken to both Morgan and Olivia. We can spend the summer there with the kids, so they can explore Europe on their own, and then the place is ours for two weeks. It'll work with our schedules since one of the hotel chains we're expanding on has three locations in France. So yes, there's work involved. Oh, and since Lex bought the chateau down the road, we've carved out some time to do some family activities, including a trip to Disneyland with all the kids."

"You did this all yourself?" I ask with an incredulous stare. "You planned this?"

He nods with a triumphant smile. "I love you, Kate. And none of this would've been possible without you by my side. You destroyed my fears and made me the man I want to be for my children. You challenged me to rise above. I love you, and I know you hate the romantic talk, but fuck it, we deserve our happily ever after, and why not experience it in a castle during the summer?"

I shake my head proudly, quick to correct him. "No, Noah, you did that all on your own. I was just standing beside you, making sure you know how strong you are."

His lips find mine, sealing our fate with a kiss. Inside his embrace, I'm exactly where I was destined to be. I have chased heartbreak, and it led me into his arms, into a life I never knew I wanted.

"So, what now?" he murmurs, burying his head into my hair.

"I love it, our own castle. It really makes the pair of socks I bought you seem less important," I tease, grabbing his hand. "If we're giving presents now, then I might as well give you yours, but just a heads up, I like it hard and fast."

Noah purses his lips, tilting his head as we step into the garage. "I hope you're talking about my cock because you've been teasing me all night in this red skirt you're wearing."

"Close your eyes," I instruct him.

"Okay, but is this why you said I wasn't allowed in the garage? You told me that a cabinet was being resprayed and no dust could settle in the room."

"I lied, and I regret nothing." I switch the light on. "Open your eyes."

Slowly, Noah opens his eyes only for them to widen in shock. "Holy shit! Is this what I think it is?"

I nod my head while grinning. "A Kawasaki Ultra, the perfect combination of performance and luxury."

His hands glide against the leather seats, admiring the watercraft in awe.

"I can't believe it," he renders speechless. "But why two?"

"You don't think that you get to have all the fun?" I place my hands on my hips. "I want the adrenaline rush, too."

Noah pulls me into him, his face lit up in joy. "You're crazy perfect, you know that?"

"Hmm, remember that when I'm kicking your ass in the water and you're pouting like a baby."

"Thank you," he murmurs, planting a soft kiss on my lips. "This is the most perfect Christmas I could've asked for. And for the record, no way you'll kick my ass. As soon as the weather warms up, we're taking them out to Newport Beach."

I turn around to pull him into the house, not wanting to

be too far away from Nash. Reluctantly, he turns off the light, slapping my ass on our way back inside.

"Movie night?" I suggest, pulling him into the living room. "A Christmas movie is a must."

Noah groans. "Okay, but it's not that one with Hugh what's-his-face, he plays the Prime Minister and falls in love with that British chick? British men are so corny."

"*Love Actually.*"

"Huh?"

I laugh while kissing him. "*Love Actually*. A Christmas classic."

"You're not going to say it's a rite into the passage of adulthood, are you?"

"Nope, prepare yourself for heartbreak, baby. Followed by all the feels."

Noah falls onto the sofa, closing his eyes while letting out a huff. I sit beside him, throwing a blanket over us. With my legs on top of his, he massages me before sliding into my shirt.

"Shall we fuck now before you ruin the movie?" I ask with a knowing smirk, my gaze fixated on the flat screen.

"If the movie was that good, I wouldn't need to fuck you," he retorts.

"You *always* need to fuck me."

Noah climbs on top of me as a knock on the door interrupts us.

"Are we expecting anyone?"

I shake my head.

Noah heads to the door and returns with a gold box. It's rather fancy with a touch of elegance.

"A delivery this late?" I question, curious.

"Someone must really want us to open a Christmas gift."

He places the box between us, ripping the bow off. Inside sits another gold box. Both of us look at each other before we open the lid and see the pearl paper. My eyes read over it until they open wide with shock.

"What is it?"

"O.M.G," I yell, jumping off the couch. *"Eric's getting married!"*

EPILOGUE

NOAH

My finger's drum tap against the large woodgrain table as the presentation plays on the large screen.

The 3D impressions of the refurbishments to one of the largest hotels we're trying to turnover is causing my mind to run at full speed. Projections, timeframes, campaigning—the list goes on.

"State-of-the-art amenities, a world-class health center, luxury dining—everything we need to stay competitive in the hotel industry," Cruz, our head project manager, concludes.

Distracted by the opulence of this thirty-million-dollar project, I haven't feasted my eyes on Kate sitting diagonally across the table. When it comes to meetings, I always try my best to ignore her, with reason.

The woman knows how to dress. Who would have thought her corporate attire would be such a fucking turn-on every goddamn day. The white dress she's wearing today with the gold pumps is doing nothing to curb my hard-on.

I'm confident, no wait, sure, I've fucked her before in this dress because it did the exact same thing to me the first time she wore it.

Shit, the stir in my pants is uncomfortable, causing me to shift my legs. *This is why you need to ignore her. Your dick is out of fucking control.*

As Cruz shifts his presentation to a less appealing subject, boredom seeps in with my mind drifting to Kate.

It's been six months since the day Kate moved here, and six months in which my life changed forever.

There is never a dull moment in our lives. Our jobs, demanding with many challenges, had me traveling interstate more than I cared to admit. According to Charlie and her ever-so unwanted opinion of my life, I had turned into Lex. It came with a lecture, of course, on work-life balance and being present for my family.

Kate, equally as dedicated to her work, rose to my defense each time. She understands exactly the kind of job we do and the responsibilities of being on the executive team. One thing I have learned working beside her—she is incredibly hard-working and an absolute shark in the boardroom. Men are intimidated by her, and although I will tease her after hours about her aggressive nature, I don't blame her one bit. In our industry, you need to play the right cards in order to win the deal.

No one messes with her.

But sitting across from me, her face is anything but aggressive, more troubled by something else demanding her attention. Her fingers are typing rapidly on her phone, brow creasing and lips tight. *Fuck, those lips look amazing wrapped against my cock.*

I check the time on my watch, noting we've gone over

and use this as an excuse to wrap up Cruz since the bastard can talk for hours.

"We need to wind this up. I've got another meeting. I'd like to see more accurate numbers we anticipate for these improvements, and Chris, can we get approval times, too? Any changes this grand will need to be submitted for development approval."

I wait to see if Kate wants to add anything, clearing my throat to catch her attention.

She lifts her head, sliding her phone away while narrowing her eyes.

"This needs to meet our deadline. We want this completed by next summer to capitalize on people vacationing. Projections people, get it to us by next Monday." Rising from her chair, she grabs her phone and notes, leaving the room abruptly without another word nor a glance my way.

Chris pulls me aside, asking me to take a look at a few things this afternoon. As soon as I'm done, I walk toward Kate's office to see her standing beside the large glass window, texting furiously.

I don't knock, closing the door behind me. Leaning against the wall, I keep my distance to remain professional in the workplace, an arduous task when the woman you love is only a few feet away, and you haven't seen her in three days due to traveling.

"You're quiet. What's wrong?"

Kate tilts her head sideways, appearing dazed until she focuses on my face.

"Noah," she softens, the tone already warning me to pay attention because it doesn't sound promising. "I just... something has come up. It's about this weekend."

Fuck my life, not this again.

This weekend is Eric and Tristan's bachelor weekend. Apparently, just one night isn't good enough, so they scheduled a whole weekend of partying—a penthouse suite at one of the hotels we've acquired, including the nightclub reserved only for their guests. Vegas brings back memories of my boys, Benny and Tom, and me in our single days with pool parties while drunk on Alizé. It feels like a whole other lifetime ago.

And perhaps, with age, my partying days seem less important. I would rather spend the entire weekend in bed, devouring my woman because that always has a happy ending.

My frustration begins to grow again, having heard nonstop about this weekend for the past few weeks. Frankly, I have more pressing things on my mind.

"What now? Eric's got a wardrobe issue, or let me guess, he can't get the right kind of champagne. There are bigger problems in the world than Eric's goddamn weekend."

Kate's stare is fixated on me, her arms crossing beneath her beautiful tits, only making them fuller.

You're distracted again. Calm the fuck down.

"Dominic is coming."

The second the name drops, anger sweeps through me like a force of nature. My fists clench into a ball, stiff against my sides as I stretch my neck in silence. Beneath the business shirt and vest I'm wearing, heat rises, making the room stifling hot.

The timing of this *man* has been the bane of my existence. The nerve of him to pursue Kate like she's a fucking toy, to turning up at her apartment begging her with his newly found profession of love. And all of a sudden, he is Eric's best friend, their bond unbreakable from the brotherhood.

I don't buy it for one second. He has an agenda, and he wants what is mine.

"Talk to me, please," she begs with pleading eyes.

"What's there to say?" I shrug, folding my arms while tucking in my upper lip. "He's Eric's brother, apparently."

"*Noah.*"

A knock on the door breaks the mounting tension. Lex enters the room quietly, watching both of us with curiosity.

"Am I interrupting anything?"

"No," we both say in unison.

"Great," he says, though still appearing cautious. "Noah, can we move our five o'clock meeting to now? Charlotte is held up across town, so I need to pick up the girls."

"Sure."

"Lex," Kate calls as she walks to her desk. "Before you leave, can you sign these documents so we can FedEx them to Manhattan overnight?"

Lex moves toward the table, grabbing a pen and signing the papers.

"I'll meet you in your office in five minutes," he tells me before leaving the room and closing the door behind him.

"My afternoon is clear, so I'm going to pick up the kids," Kate mentions once he is gone.

"I thought Morgan had Jessa tonight, and we only had Nash?"

"Morgan texted me an hour ago. Her flight is delayed, and she won't be in until after eight. You know Jessa is always exhausted on Fridays after school. I suggested she stay the night and pick her up in the morning before we leave for Vegas."

The guilt consumes me, the anger I momentarily take out on Kate because I can't control Dominic attending this weekend. And she doesn't deserve my anger, not when she's done everything she can possibly do to make our family work. She is the reason why Morgan and I can finally co-parent without the hateful words and threats. She's also the reason why my son is in my life more than ever.

"A good idea," I mumble, defeated. "I'll see you tonight once I'm done."

She nods her head in agreeance. "And Noah?"

"Yeah."

"I love you. Just a bump, okay? We'll get through this because we always do."

Inside my office, Lex is already sitting down while talking on his phone. His tone is unforgiving, and judging by the way he is pinching the bridge of his nose, he is not getting the answers he needs.

"Just get me those signed contracts you promised to deliver. You've got until the close of business."

He ends the call abruptly as I've seen him do several times before, letting out a puff of air while shaking his head in annoyance.

"Let's call Johnson. I'm certain he will come up with some excuse as to why he is late with his numbers," I mention, frustrated at dealing with idiots.

"Before we do that, is everything okay? Between you and Kate?"

"It's fine," I lie, not wanting to get into the semantics of it all.

"I heard about Dominic. Charlotte told me this afternoon."

I crack my neck, the sound of his name becoming this trigger I can't seem to get any control over.

"Take it from me," Lex suggests, his brotherly advice always wise. "You're going to drive yourself crazy if you don't control the situation yourself. It's not easy to be in the company of someone who wants what you have."

"Right," I mumble. "I guess you would know since that person married your sister. Though you seem to be fine with it."

Lex lets out a long-winded breath. "I wasn't fine with it. It was a challenging time for our family. I was angry for a long time, but in the end, I had no choice. Adriana is my blood. I will do anything for her, even if that means I have to relinquish my own demons and give her freedom to make her own decisions. I guess, in the end, she is happy, and he's proven his worth."

"I don't know how you do it. The mere thought of being in the same room as that fucker, I just want to punch his fucking lights out."

A small laugh escapes Lex. "I have my moments, trust me. I'm not perfect."

Pulling my drawer open, I reach in and grab the navy velvet box and place it on the table.

"I've been carrying this for months, even before she officially moved to LA. I bought it in Paris, the night after we... you know... I want to ask Kate to marry me."

"So why haven't you? You will make my life easier since Charlotte is waiting with bated breath for this to happen. Her words, not mine."

"Because of life. We're both so busy with work, traveling, then there was the move, plus trying to balance the kids. It's been nonstop, and then you add all the goddamn nonsense of this weekend. I don't want to think I'm just doing it just because we live together."

"Of course, it's understandable. You want it to be perfect. You know, our trip to France is in two weeks. The girls are excited to finally see their castle."

"Yeah, I know. We're looking forward to it. I know Kate has been desperate to finally get there and start tearing the inside apart."

"Look, you'll know when it's right, and it's going to be perfect no matter what because you're marrying the woman you love," he says wisely. "As for this weekend, keep your distance from Dominic but always remain one step ahead. Try to refrain from punching his face because no matter what the scenario, you'll be to blame if you act first."

I nod my head, sliding the box back into the drawer and closing it.

"Let's make this call," I tell him. "We need to get this sorted out before the weekend."

I close the front door behind me, the aroma of home relaxing my tense muscles. Only a short distance away, I hear the chatter from the living room. I head to the room with small quiet steps but stop short of entering as I lean against the arch and watch quietly.

Kate is sitting on the floor, still in her work attire, but her hair is loose and her shoes removed. She always looks beautiful whether she is dressed in designer clothing or in a pair of sweats with a messy bun. But there is nothing sexier than the sight of her with my children.

Jessa is sitting beside her, brushing her doll's hair, while Nash is between her legs, trying to eat the doll's hair. The kid puts everything in his mouth. The second I make my appearance with a slight sound, Jessa's eyes lift, shining so bright as she runs to me. I throw her into my arms, smelling her hair before kissing her forehead.

"Daddy, why are you so late?"

Jesus, talk about guilt, kid.

"I had to work, princess."

Placing her down, she runs back to Kate, so I take Nash in my arms before leaning in to kiss Kate's lips, giving her space to stretch her legs.

When it comes to the kids, Kate's patience amazes me. She makes our family dynamic work so effortlessly, and given she's never experienced living with children, she takes the time to learn, and I couldn't do any of this without her.

Even more the reason to make her your wife.

"The kids are fed, bathed, and ready for bed soon." Kate yawns, her normally vibrant eyes appearing tired. "As am I. It's been a long day."

We play with the kids a little while longer before we commence the grueling task of bedtime. Nash is much easier—the kid is knocked out by the lullaby's second verse which plays in his room—but Jessa is much more demanding. She loves to read and will embellish the stories to drag it out, finding any excuse not to go to sleep.

After reading three stories and reminding her about the trip to the zoo with Morgan and Callum tomorrow, she finally agrees for me to leave the room but not until Kate comes to say good night.

We swap roles, Kate taking over while I head to our room and straight for the shower. The hot water is relaxing every part of me, though a blow job would be perfect right now. Three nights of sleeping alone in a hotel room is doing *nothing* to curb my fucking dick right now.

Knowing Jessa tends to walk into our room about a thousand times before she finally falls asleep, I place on my boxers and exit the bathroom to see Kate pulling down the zipper of her dress.

Standing behind her, I move her hair away from her

neck and plant a kiss on her shoulder, inhaling her skin which smells like coconut from the body lotion she wears.

"Go check on Jessa," Kate suggests. "I'll take a shower."

I slap her ass softly before going to check on Jessa. Surprisingly, she is fast asleep, already snoring.

Back in the room, I climb into bed and wait for Kate to finish. She exits the bathroom dressed in a black satin nightie which sits so far up her thigh I can practically see her beautiful pussy begging to be tasted. When she climbs into bed and turns off the lamp, I pull her body to mine and run my hand up her nightie to her breasts as she strokes my hair.

My words fall silent as I think about my behavior this afternoon, but I can't lose her.

She is my life.

"Noah, I know you're angry, but this is life. We can't avoid our past. Lord knows it's a heavy lesson learned these past six months."

"But it's different. Morgan and Olivia don't pine for me."

"Pine? Really, we're using that word?"

I sit up, pulling my hand away. "In guy's language, he still jerks off thinking about you, and no doubt he'll tell you this weekend how great it was when he was inside you. How you'll come back to him because you can't resist."

"Noah." She breathes with a slight ache. "He can say whatever the hell he wants. The only person I want is the man beside me when he's not being a dick."

"I hate him."

"I know."

"Why couldn't you have been a virgin? That would have made my life easier."

"I doubt it. I laid there extremely quiet from memory

and stared at the ceiling, counting down the seconds until it was over. I was seventeen at the time and didn't have sex again until I was twenty."

"You would have if it was with me."

Kate kisses my hair softly, reassuring me as she has done several times before. I hate being jealous, but the woman turns heads wherever she goes, and it riles me every time men devour her with their eyes.

"We'll never know. But Noah, you've got to deal with the fact that this may not be the only time we see him. There's the wedding for starters. While I'm surprised how close they have become, I can't not be a part of Eric's life because of my past. Granted, it was a fucked-up decision on my part, but it's done."

"It annoys me that you're rational, just so you know."

"One of us has to be." She snickers as I jab my finger into her side, playfully. "No one will ever change the way I feel about you. This is our life now, our family, and whether you like it or not, you're stuck with me."

I climb on top of her, running my thumb against her bottom lip. "I'd die a happy man to be stuck with you for life. But for now, it's been three nights since I've been inside of you."

Kate raises her lips, lingering on mine as I graze my teeth causing her to shiver beside me. "Well, what are you waiting for?"

Our bodies move in sync, the way it has always been. I can't get enough of her wild, insatiable ways, though she blames me for being the sex maniac. I've finally met my match in the bedroom. Kate enjoys kink when we are in an empty house and can fuck against every surface, and I love her even more because of it.

I bury myself inside her, knowing I can't hold back—the

pleasure floods my entire body and drives me to the brink of insanity. We silence our moans, careful not to wake the kids until I pull out and lay on my back, demanding she climb on top. As she slides herself on, I pull the strap of her nighty down, exposing her tits. She's beautiful, and soon, she's going to be your wife if you can get off your ass and fucking seal the deal.

Arching her back, she rides me faster until her body tenses, and I feel her coming all over my cock. *Fuck.* I grab her hips while my body shakes, and the dark room becomes a burst of light, my heart pounding so hard, making it impossible to ignore.

"Oh fuck," I groan, barely able to breathe.

Kate falls on top of me, her heaving chest beating against my own. Barely able to move, I stroke her hair as we lay quietly, both of us trying to calm down. "Why can't we stay here all weekend? Just you and me."

"Because Eric deserves this. Besides, it's Vegas, baby. Pool parties and chicks in bikinis. Isn't this your fantasy?"

"I believe my fantasy was fulfilled two weeks ago when you gave me the most intense blow job in the elevator."

Kate laughs against my chest. "We have to stop sneaking around, or we'll get busted."

"Please, you think Lex is so innocent?" I remind her. "You know what, don't answer that."

"I know for a fact he isn't. Remember, Charlie is my best friend and doesn't hold back on information."

"I hope that sentiment isn't returned," I deadpan, closing my eyes to catch a moment's rest. "Have you forgotten she's my cousin?"

"No, I have not. Which is why I keep our sex life private."

"Hang on, but you and Adriana are tight."

"Ah yes..." she whispers, though I hear the smile on her voice. "Her and Julian... wow."

"What do you mean, wow? Better than us?"

"Oh, baby." Kate raises her eyes to meet mine, her face still visible from the slightly open drapes. "No one is better than us. But just to be sure, maybe you should remind me again?"

"You're crazy."

"That's why you love me, right?"

I cup her face to kiss her lips. "On all fours, now."

We barely slept, having spent the night devouring each other like it was our first time. We fell asleep just before dawn, only for Nash to wake up like clockwork at six. Allowing Kate some extra time to sleep, I change Nash's diaper and take him downstairs for breakfast. Jessa follows soon after, eager for her trip to the zoo.

Kate isn't one to sleep in much, always an early riser, something we have in common. Already dressed for our road trip in a pair of tiny black shorts and this off-the-shoulder denim blouse, I comment on seeing her ass cheeks, and she argues for me to get over myself.

Olivia arrives early, picking Nash up to spend the weekend with him until we take him off her hands on Tuesday. She stays for a coffee, chatting with Kate as they laugh about something I choose not to listen to. Surprisingly, the two of them have become great friends. They have a lot in common, enjoy the same things, and I don't complain since it makes my life easier.

Not long after she leaves, Morgan arrives. Things between us are a lot better. We communicate without the heated exchanges, but we aren't exactly friends. She spends more time talking to Kate than me, but I don't give a shit. As long as Jessa is happy, that's all that matters.

"You ready to go?" I ask once everyone leaves, throwing the last suitcase in the car. "Our flight leaves in an hour."

"Ready to get wasted Vegas-style," she cheers while hopping into the car.

~

We fly the private plane with Lex, Charlie, Adriana, and Julian. Eric and Tristan are already in Vegas, and Rocky and Nikki are flying in from New York.

The flight takes less than an hour, and in that hour, all the alcohol on the plane has been consumed. We do rounds of shots, plan how we can torment Eric in Vegas, and make the weekend unforgettable.

By midday, we arrive at the hotel, ready to check-in. Each couple goes their separate ways, all of us agreeing to meet in an hour inside the lobby.

"What can we do in an hour?" I whisper into Kate's ear as she attempts to fill out our details on the check-in form. "Blow job, then anal?"

Kate shakes her head with a knowing smirk. "Dirty boy, and we both know you're greedy, so let's see if we even get there since you seem to linger on the deep throat."

"Your gag reflex is perfect," I tease, my hands gliding against the small of her back. "If it wasn't so good, I wouldn't beg for more."

"Cue the sweet talk. We know I'm good, so stop distracting me, so I can wrap my mouth around that beautiful cock of yours."

I grab her hand, ignoring the people around us, and pull

her toward the elevators. As soon as the door opens, I'm about to press the button to stop anyone else from entering, so I can slide my fingers into her shorts to feel how wet she is until the doors ping open.

"Well, if it isn't the happy couple."

The sound of his voice blinds me with an uncontrollable rage. I'm caught off-guard, unprepared to deal with this motherfucker and his annoying presence. I stretch my neck, my nostrils flaring as Kate squeezes my hand. I don't look his way, unwilling to give him the satisfaction of my attention.

"Dominic, how are you?"

"Fine, Kate."

"That's good to hear," she says politely before continuing, "Listen, I love Eric. I don't want there to be animosity between us when we're all here for him and Tristan."

Dominic keeps his attention fixated on the door. "Yes, we're all here for Eric. There is nothing more important to me than the bond of brotherhood. And he is your best friend, correct?"

I'm about to punch his fucking face, swallowing the anger as Kate tightens her grip on me. But I keep quiet, remembering Lex's words. Always remain one step ahead. If he wants to pull the brotherhood card out, I will keep a close eye, knowing he has a hidden angle in trying to stay close to Kate.

The door pings open as we reach our floor. *Fuck, finally.*

"Now, if you'll excuse us, we need to get ready for tonight. I guess we'll see you later."

Kate drags us out, but I stop her, holding the door as my eyes blaze against his. For the longest time, I envied this man for having been the attention of my best friend. But as I continue to stare into the eyes of my enemy, I see nothing but a sad, pathetic man, who creates a world based on false fantasies and ruins people's self-worth for his own selfish needs.

"It'll be in your best interest to remember that this weekend is about your brother and nothing else," I warn him in an arctic tone. "Do you understand me?"

The dickhead smirks like a fucking idiot, though behind his complacent façade, I see the blaze out of control because the woman he loves walks away so easily.

"I'll see you soon, Kate," is all he says while we battle with our stare.

The doors close at the same time. Kate pulls me toward the room and unlocks the door. The second we are inside, I kick the goddamn chair, angered by what I knew all along.

"Noah, you have to let it go."

I slide the balcony door open, relishing in the fresh air to calm me down. My hands grip the railing as I stare at the view of the strip below me.

"Let it go?" A sinister laugh escapes me while I shake my head. "Right."

"What the hell is wrong with you?" Kate raises her voice behind me. "I get it, I really do. But you've said over and over again that you know how much I love you, so what else is it? Because it's starting to sound like you don't trust me, and if that's the truth, that's a whole other argument, especially since I'm the one who has had to compromise for you and have your exes in our lives for the sake of the kids."

"I trust you," I confess, almost raising my voice, frustrated at my own insecurities. "I just want a moment to get down on one knee and make you my wife. That perfect moment to prove to you how much I want us to be husband

and wife. And everyone in our lives demands so much of us, I can barely fuck you let alone propose marriage to you."

"What if there isn't such a thing as a perfect moment? You can always plan, but sometimes, that perfect moment is spontaneous. There's no thought, just careless thoughts carrying us away like our dip in the ocean that night. Whatever may have happened afterward, our crazy actions led us to bond in a jail cell. And look at us now."

"I guess so," I mumble. "I hadn't thought of it that way."

"Noah." I turn around as she inches closer, placing her hand on my cheek, caressing it softly. "We are not ordinary. And that's what makes our bond unique. We're not Charlie or Lex or even Adriana and Julian. We are Noah and Kate. Two best friends who fell apart four years ago and got through the hardest years of our lives to end up here, together. Our love story is far from perfect, but it's perfect for me."

"I'm sorry, and you're right. I just hate how much he crawls under my skin."

"It's called jealousy." She smiles, her arms around me. "So back to the whole wife thing..."

"Yeah," I grin, "I've never hidden the fact that I want all of you, mine forever."

"Let's just get married, here, tonight."

"Here?" I tilt my head, questioning her. "In Vegas?"

"Why not?"

"I just thought you'd want the whole big wedding. Didn't you spend your whole childhood dreaming about being a bride?"

Kate laughs. "Uh, no. I had two brothers. I jumped out of trees and played in the dirt. Sorry to burst your bubble, I'm not Charlie. We've spent our time together worrying about everyone else, Noah, so let's have this. Just us."

"I didn't think I could love you more, but... I love you more." Happiness bursts through me, my hands cupping her face to bring her kiss into me. "I want to marry you tonight."

"Then, what the hell are we waiting for? But I do have one condition."

"Me, too. You go first."

"I think we should still have something small back home to include Jessa and Nash."

I laugh, shaking my head. "That was my condition, too."

"And see, this is why it pays to be best friends first." She smiles, arms wrapped around my neck. "I'm so ready to marry you, Noah Mason."

"Then, let's fucking do it," I tell her, grinning. "I need to finally make you my wife."

The church is tiny and cheap with plastic stained windows instead of glass and pink neon lights inside the confined space. Instead of wooden pews like a traditional church, tacky velvet benches run across the room. It's a typical Vegas chapel just like out of the movies with a shiny tiled floor and old cigarette smoke smell.

Kate wears a white laced jumpsuit, and I, the navy suit I brought with me for tonight. She looks radiant like a bride on her wedding day despite it being less formal.

Inside the chapel, in front of Elvis, the organist who looks well into her nineties, plus Lex and Charlie, I pull out the box from my pocket and get down on one knee.

"I want a sign, something to tell me this is exactly the right moment." I clear my throat, choking on my words. "I know we agreed to get married, and at that moment only an hour ago, it felt right. But when you left the room to get changed with Charlie, I remembered this inside my bag. I've carried it everywhere hoping for a sign, but I realized I was chasing something when all along, it was inside of me. I can't imagine my life without you. The way you make me laugh, the crazy adventures we experience together. You've welcomed my children as if they were your own. We've made memories because you are never afraid of living life to the fullest. And because of that, you've made me a better person."

I open the box as Kate gasps in front of me.

"*Je t'aime. Épouse-moi, Kate.*"

I pull out the Cartier platinum-cut oval diamond ring and slide it on her finger. I repeat my sentiments. "I love you. Marry me, Kate."

"A thousand times yes," she bursts out, smiling as her eyes glaze over. "*Tu es parfait pour moi, Noah.*"

And that's the thing about love. When the person you breathe for tells you that you're perfect to them, it's the only thing that matters.

"Let's rock n' roll and get this show on the road!" Elvis cheers.

Charlie squeals beside us, clutching onto Lex as he grins while holding onto her.

We say our I do's, and finally, I make my best friend my wife.

I stare into the eyes of this beautiful woman, my smile just as infectious as hers, and lift her hand with the newly appointed wedding ring which sits next to her diamond ring.

"To us... my best friend, my equal."

"To us." Kate grins with her big blue eyes shining bright. "I can't believe we're married!"

"We have done some pretty crazy things, but this one takes the cake."

"You guys." Charlie hugs both of us at the same time. "I've been waiting forever for this to happen. Congratulations, I love you both."

Lex pulls me in for a hug, then onto Kate as Charlie holds both my hands. "I promised you a happy ending before we left for Paris. I knew deep down inside you that leading you back to Kate would be the road to happiness."

"Yeah, you're kinda annoying that way?" I laugh before pulling her in and squeezing her tight.

"So, now that you're married, what's the first thing you want to do?" Charlie asks.

Lex shakes his head, covering his laugh. "What's the first thing we did?"

"Oh," Charlie mouths. "Never mind."

I pull Kate into me, wrapping my arms around her waist. "How about you give me two hours to devour my wife and then we'll join you? Are you ready to watch two gay men squirm at a strip joint?"

"Eric hates pussy." Lex chuckles.

Inside my pocket, I retrieve a bundle of bills. "I'm ready with my bills so Eric gets the full experience. Pussy galore in his face. I guess, payback for all the shit he's put me through."

Kate pulls more bills out of her purse. "Here, I'll double that. I say we get the ladies to tag team him."

We all laugh until Lex pulls out his black Amex. "This one is on me."

"You guys are so bad." Charlie shakes her head with a devilish smirk. "And I'm here for every second of it, shall we?"

I grab the hand of my wife, my best friend.

"Let's get this party started."

THE END

You are invited to Eric and Tristan's wedding.
To accept your invitation and enjoy the bonus chapters
from all your favorite characters,
make sure you subscribe to my newsletter.

ALSO BY KAT T. MASEN

The Dark Love Series

Featuring Lex & Charlie

Chasing Love: A Billionaire Love Triangle

Chasing Us: A Second Chance Love Triangle

Chasing Her: A Stalker Romance

Chasing Him: A Forbidden Second Chance Romance

Chasing Fate: An Enemies-to-Lovers Romance

Chasing Heartbreak: A Friends-to-Lovers Romance

The Forbidden Love Series

(Dark Love Series Second Generation)

Featuring Amelia Edwards

The Trouble With Love: An Age Gap Romance

The Trouble With Us: A Second Chance Love Triangle

The Trouble With Him: A Secret Pregnancy Romance

The Trouble With Her: A Friends-to-Lovers Romance

The Trouble With Fate: An Enemies-to-Lovers Romance

Also by Kat T. Masen

The Office Rival: An Enemies-to-Lovers Romance

The Marriage Rival: An Office Romance

Bad Boy Player: A Brother's Best Friend Romance

Roomie Wars Box Set (Books 1 to 3): Friends-to-Lovers Series

ABOUT THE AUTHOR

Born and bred in Sydney, Australia, **Kat T. Masen** is a mother to four crazy boys and wife to one sane husband. Growing up in a generation where social media and fancy gadgets didn't exist, she enjoyed reading from an early age and found herself immersed in these stories. After meeting friends on Twitter who loved to read as much as she did, her passion for writing began, and the friendships continued on despite the distance.

"I'm known to be crazy and humorous. Show me the most random picture of a dog in a wig, and I'll be laughing for days."

Download free bonus content, purchase signed paperbacks & bookish merchandise.

Visit: **www.kattmasen.com**

Made in the USA
Middletown, DE
05 October 2023

40232090R00175